TRACING YOUR YORKSHIRE ANCESTORS

TRACING YOUR YORKSHIRE ANCESTORS

RACHEL BELLERBY

Pen & Sword
FAMILY HISTORY

To David and Erin, my inspiration

First published in Great Britain in 2006 by
PEN & SWORD FAMILY HISTORY
an imprint of
Pen & Sword Books Ltd
47 Church Street
Barnsley
South Yorkshire
S70 2AS

ISBN 1 84415 468 8

A CIP catalogue record for this book is
available from the British Library.

Typeset in Palatino and Optima by
Phoenix Typesetting, Auldgirth, Dumfriesshire

Printed and bound in England by
Biddles Ltd, Kings Lynn

Pen & Sword Books Ltd incorporates the Imprints of
Pen & Sword Aviation, Pen & Sword Maritime, Pen & Sword Military,
Wharncliffe Local History, Pen & Sword Select, Pen & Sword Military
Classics and Leo Cooper.

For a complete list of Pen & Sword titles please contact
PEN & SWORD BOOKS LIMITED
47 Church Street, Barnsley, South Yorkshire, S70 2AS, England
E-mail: enquiries@pen-and-sword.co.uk
Website: www.pen-and-sword.co.uk

CONTENTS

INTRODUCTION

Yorkshire is one of the UK's most diverse counties, with a fascinating and varied history stretching back thousands of years. Yorkshire men and women such as Captain James Cook, the Bronte sisters, and Thomas Chippendale have made their mark and, whilst we cannot all claim such illustrious forebears, our own ancestors also played their part in Yorkshire's history and many have left behind tantalizing evidence of their existence.

It is relatively simple to find out when our ancestors were born, married and died. But what about those years in between? How can we find out more about the childhoods, working and social lives of our ancestors? This book will give you dozens of ideas about how to find out more about those names on your family tree. Yorkshire is home to some excellent archives, some of them little known, and these archives can be found in the most unexpected places. The following chapters will help kick-start your research and bring what were once just names to vivid life.

YORKSHIRE'S ARCHIVES

Archives are records relating to all aspects of society. Records that we, when researching our family history, find so useful, such as censuses and hearth taxes, were actually compiled and retained for administrative and governmental purposes. The records referred to throughout this book take many different forms. Many people think of archives as dusty volumes of leather-bound books. But there are many different forms of archive materials, as we shall discover. The material referred to throughout the

Thomas Chippendale, one of Yorkshire's most famous residents.

following chapters will include paper-based sources such as censuses, wills and letters, visual material such as maps and photographs and, finally, more modern forms of archive material such as films and sound recordings.

It can be quite daunting making your first visit to a particular record office, archive or local studies library, especially if you are not quite sure what you are looking for, or even exactly what type of records are held there. This book aims to help you to discover what you will find where, how the records you will come across in your research can help you and where to find further information. Not only will we look at places which hold records that might not yet be familiar to you, we will also find out how you can use the records held at traditional archive repositories in different ways. There is much more to family history research than birth, marriage, death and census records.

Of course, it would be impossible to begin any family history research without referring to traditional sources such as censuses and birth certificates. Such items are the bare bones of tracing your ancestry. But they are only the starting point. Once you have gathered some of these documents you can really begin to make sense of your research by putting the information you have into context.

Contained within the book's chapters are several case studies. These cover in some detail collections or groups of documents which are felt to be of particular use and relevance. The case studies show you how to use bare facts and make them into something relevant to your own research interests; bringing your own family's past to life.

Anyone living in Yorkshire is fortunate in that the county is home to some of the UK's most important archives. These include the Borthwick Institute of Historical Research at York, a major archive specializing in ecclesiastical history, which holds centuries' worth of records for the county. The registry of deeds at Wakefield can also be very important to family history researchers, as we shall see later.

Various archives and museums are mentioned by name at different points throughout the book, in cases where they can assist in different research topics. All institutions mentioned in the book are listed in chapter 10 with full contact and website details. Most of the archives referred to throughout this book have their own websites. These sites can be an excellent way to begin research, as they usually give a good overview of the research material available, any conditions of access and new accessions are often added regularly.

Though the websites cannot be a substitute for an actual visit to the archive, they can help you to prepare for your visit beforehand, helping you to get the best out of your research time by pinpointing what type of material you would like to see.

We will explore the places that will take you on a journey to discover your ancestors and find out about how they lived. You might be lucky enough to unearth a famous ancestor, find a photograph of a relative, even read about your ancestors in a newspaper. One thing is for sure, once you have begun searching the archives the county of Yorkshire has to offer, you will want to find out more and more.

ACCESS TO ARCHIVES

If I could only recommend one website to anyone tracing their family history in Yorkshire, it would be the Access to Archives website. It has been invaluable to me in researching this book and I believe there is no better place on the internet for finding out where various Yorkshire records are kept. The website address is www.a2a.org.uk If you have never used the site, give it a try and you will quickly find it an invaluable research tool.

The 'search the database' section on the website is the main way to access the catalogues contained in the site. Access to Archives allows all the country's archives, museums and other institutions that hold records to catalogue their holdings for everyone to view. Clicking on to the 'search the database' section allows you to select data using a keyword, a particular archive repository or an English region, or a combination of these.

For example, typing in the keywords 'Captain James Cook' and selecting the English region 'Yorkshire' brings up three selections. These separate groups of records are held at Bradford Archives, Hull University library and the Whitby Literary and Philosophical Society; three very different types of archive repositories. Clicking on each choice reveals more about the records that are held and their catalogue number, should you wish to visit the archive to see the materials. Once in this section, clicking on the name of the archive office brings up full contact details, usually including opening times and conditions of access.

Alternatively, selecting an archive, in this example Otley Museum, brings up nine catalogues. These include school records for several local schools, dating from 1883, Otley Parish Church records from 1684 and various archives for local businesses. Any of these could possibly be used in research for an ancestor who lived in the town. Although the Access to Archives website often has fairly brief catalogue descriptions, because of the vast amount of information held on the site, as a way to pinpoint quickly where archives are held, it is unparalleled.

BEGINNING YOUR SEARCH

There are many excellent books on family history and genealogy; this book does not attempt to replicate the information they hold. Instead, it aims to offer ideas to allow you start your own research projects, taking you down avenues you might not otherwise have considered.

The best place to begin a search is at home, that is, by speaking to relatives and friends who have been involved with your family. They will give you clues as to where you might start to look for material to fill out your family history research. Living relatives can be invaluable in filling in the gaps of your own knowledge.

After this, the county record offices probably hold much of the most important material for beginning to chart your family history. But the search does not stop there. Items held at county record offices such as censuses, parish registers and even birth, marriage and death indexes can take you far. But what they cannot do is put flesh on the bones. And that is what we will be attempting to do in the course of this book.

You can be sure of a warm Yorkshire welcome in any of the places featured in *Tracing Your Yorkshire Ancestors*. All of the people contacted were happy to help me find out information and many went out of their way to assist. Archives are there for us to use, and a visit to any of the places mentioned in this book could start you on a quest for knowledge that will last a lifetime.

HOW THE COUNTY OF YORKSHIRE WAS ORGANIZED

Before being administratively reorganized in 1974, Yorkshire was the largest county in England. It was made up of three ridings; North, East and West, and divided into administrative units called wapentakes. Two major places not included in the wapentake system were York and Kingston upon Hull.

When the county was reorganized in 1974, many records were transferred to the new authorities, where they can still be found today. The main areas which hold information on both the modern county and the older ridings are: Cleveland, Humberside, North Yorkshire, South Yorkshire and West Yorkshire.

York had never been part of the ridings, but was classed as a county in its own right. Northallerton had been the capital of the North Riding and it is here that the North Yorkshire county record office is based.

In this book, we will explore dozens of different archive repositories. These can be broadly grouped into categories, which are outlined below. You may not use all of them to begin with, particularly if you have just begun to trace your family history. But it is interesting to discover what kind of material is held where, so that you have an idea of the places that may be able to further your search.

COUNTY RECORD OFFICES

Many English counties have only one county record office, but the situation is different in Yorkshire. The East Riding and North Yorkshire areas both have county record offices, at Beverley and Northallerton respectively, with the cities of Hull and York having their own city archives.

West Yorkshire is covered by the West Yorkshire Archive Service, which has branches in Bradford, Halifax, Huddersfield, Leeds and headquarters at Wakefield. South Yorkshire has archives provided by each district council, which are Barnsley, Sheffield and Rotherham.

There are also two institutions which serve the whole county: the Borthwick Institute of Historical Research at York and the Yorkshire Archaeological Society at Leeds, which was established during the nineteenth century as a repository for archives long before the county record offices were conceived.

After getting as much family information as possible, the county record office is a valuable next step in your research. As we shall see, the record office that covers the place where your ancestors lived will be able to provide you with access to materials potentially covering the lives of many of your ancestors. You may be able to find a record of their baptism in a parish register, read a log book from the school they went to, access business records for their place of employment and read about their sporting prowess in a local newspaper.

UNIVERSITY ARCHIVES

Many people overlook the possibility of carrying out research in university archives, perhaps believing that these are only open to students at the facilities. At the majority of universities this is not the case and personal researchers are welcome by appointment.

Yorkshire's universities hold many important archive collections. Historically, the universities have received bequests and donations of archive materials. This may be because of a link that a particular person had with the institution, either as a student, professor or honorary fellow. Alternatively, a particular university may specialize in certain subjects and the items donated reflect this fact. Or the person donating the material may have felt that the students at the university would benefit from the archives being available for research on the premises.

Most of the archive collections held in the region's universities are catalogued on the Access to Archives website. By using the main 'search' facility, it is possible to enter the institution of interest and see a complete catalogue of items held in their archives. Alternatively, you can search by name, place or subject.

Another useful website is www.archiveshub.ac.uk This site provides information about thousands of archive collections in the UK's universities and colleges. It is possible to type in a keyword and results are returned, giving a description of the actual archive collection, what it consists of and where it is held. For example, typing in the town name Whitby brings up 49 records.

These include papers for shipping magnate George Buckton, held at Hull University library.

It is also possible to carry out a search by selecting the name of a Yorkshire institution. Selecting 'Huddersfield University' brought up ten records, including records of the mechanics' institution 1843–84 and the archives of the Huddersfield Female Educational Institute for 1846–83.

MUSEUM ARCHIVES

In the UK, we are fortunate in having hundreds of museums in our cities, towns and villages, devoted to preserving and presenting the past. There are museums covering many British traditions from sailing to sewing, from railways to reading. What many people don't realize is that much of the material held by these museums is actually kept behind the scenes in museum archives.

This book will explore some of these museums and what they have to offer the family history researcher. By making an appointment, it is often possible to visit museum archives and have access to photographs, artefacts and documents that are not on view to the general public. Items such as diaries, newspaper cuttings and first-hand historical accounts of various events are just some of the archives available that might not be found anywhere else.

Remember that, in archives, record offices and libraries, what you see in the public areas is only the beginning. Most of the archives are kept behind the scenes and can be viewed after consulting catalogues or asking for advice. Don't be afraid to ask staff for help. They work with the archive materials every day, have an in-depth knowledge of what records are ideal for your search and take a pride in helping you make the most of your visit.

BUSINESS ARCHIVES

Yorkshire has been home to hundreds of industries during the last few hundred years and housed numerous businesses and organizations that employed our ancestors. Many of these people will have left their mark at some point during their years of work and searching business records can be a rewarding way of finding out more about how our relatives spent their working lives.

Businesses such as Rowntrees of York and Burtons Tailors were household names and took a pride in treating their employees well. Their meticulous record keeping and the documents that have been preserved can be used for your own research, as we will see in Chapter 1.

REGISTRY OF DEEDS, WAKEFIELD

The Registry of Deeds in Wakefield, West Yorkshire, is one of the foremost resources for family history researchers in the county. The registry holds over three hundred years' worth of records on individual houses, shops and businesses in the county as they passed from hand to hand.

The property deeds at the registry can be used either to trace the history of a particular property through the years, tracking who lived there and for how many years, or to find out information about an ancestor, including how long they were at a property, who they bought it from and sold it to, and how much land the estate comprised.

Only three other counties had a registry of deeds (East Riding of Yorkshire, North Riding of Yorkshire and Middlesex) and the Wakefield registry holds around six million deeds, bound in over 12,000 volumes.

The registry is based in the same building as the headquarters of the West Yorkshire Archive Service. The deeds are open to anyone to use by appointment, and cover the period between 1704 and 1970. Property deeds can be a valuable resource to anyone researching the history of a house, farm or business but there are certain difficulties in using the deeds, which will be explained in Chapter 3, when we examine ways of tracing an ancestor through property and estate records.

THE BORTHWICK INSTITUTE OF HISTORICAL RESEARCH

Anyone carrying out family history research on Yorkshire ancestors will find the services offered by the Borthwick Institute invaluable. The Borthwick is one of the biggest archives outside London and has been established for over fifty years. It is located in purpose-built accommodation at the University of York. The Borthwick holds the majority of pre-1857 probate records for the county. The probate records include wills, inventories and administration bonds. Most of the probate registers are on microfilm.

Wills are an excellent resource, as a will not only lists the property owned by the deceased, but can contain much information about family and friends, by listing who the property was being left to. Until 1857, it was the responsibility of Church of England courts to prove wills. The 1857 Probate Act transferred this responsibility to a Court of Probate. Most Yorkshire wills proved before this Act came into place are held at the Borthwick. There is an index to these wills at the Wakefield branch of West Yorkshire Archives. The Leeds office also holds a much smaller number of records of probate, for the eastern deaneries of the archdeaconry of Richmond and some of the 'peculier' areas, including Masham and Knaresborough. A peculiar was an area which for administrative purposes was treated separately to the surrounding areas.

The Borthwick Institute is based at the University of York.

From 1858, the probate system was centralized and some large towns and cities housed district probate registries, with a principal probate registry in London. All of these registries hold copies of an annual index of wills and a copy is also held at the Wakefield Branch of West Yorkshire Archives.

Administrations were used when a person had died without making a will. In these cases, a person would be appointed to swear that they would deal with the deceased person's estate honestly and pay their creditors. The person could be a relative, friend or even a person who was owed money from the estate.

These records are kept in York probate act books and are in Latin until 1732. Much of the language in them is highly formulaic, with the same official words and phrases being used with each case. Because the York courts did not require an inventory of the deceased person's goods, these appear only rarely in the surviving records.

The probate act books also contain details of cases where wills had been left and proved, i.e. a probate act. These differ from administrations as the names of executors are mentioned. These can provide valuable clues to those who were close to the deceased and who the person who had died felt could be trusted to administer the estate after their death.

If there is one overriding message of the book it is this; the best way to discover your Yorkshire ancestors is to make your own programme of research. Follow up on things that interest you, set your own pace; you can make the research as time-consuming or as leisurely as you like. Never before have we had such a wealth of archive information available to us, both in traditional forms and through newer media such as the internet, with new and useful websites appearing every year.

Chapter 1

MAKING A LIVING: LAND AND SEA

Yorkshire's diverse landscape, ranging from windswept moorland to thriving industrial towns has meant that the county has been home to hundreds of industries over the years. So many people have Yorkshire ancestors because of the fact that the county has been such a magnet

Yorkshire's diverse landscape ranges from huge textile mills to stone-built manor houses (Manor House Museum, Ilkley).

Religious houses such as Fountains Abbey employed dozens of local people.

for people seeking employment from around the country and further afield.

The four areas of the county – North, South, East and West Yorkshire – have traditionally been known for very different specialist industries. Of course, no industry was exclusive to one geographical area, but particular regions did have their own specialist trades and sometimes whole towns or villages were dominated by one particular industry, such as mining or textiles.

North Yorkshire has been known for farming and agriculture, largely due to

Many South Yorkshire industries were 'heavy' trades such as mining and engineering.

the vast estates such as Fountains Abbey, which employed hundreds of local people in agricultural labour. South Yorkshire has a tradition of 'heavy' industries such as mining, engineering and the manufacture of steel. East Yorkshire, with its coastal towns, is known for fishing and other marine industries and West Yorkshire was known worldwide for textile production.

The records of the respective areas reflect these specializations and we will look at these more closely in the first three chapters of this book.

THE GEOGRAPHY OF THE COUNTY

The diversity contained within Yorkshire's landscape is immense. From the vast tracts of agricultural land that make up great estates such as Fountains Abbey in North Yorkshire to the quaint fishing ports of East Yorkshire; from the textile towns of West Yorkshire to the coal mines of South Yorkshire, most of the UK's main industries are represented within the county.

Although Yorkshire has a strong farming tradition, particularly in the north of the area, it has been more well known for heavy industries that mostly employed males. These included mining, fishing and engineering. Such trades often involved whole communities and so when trade was slack, an entire town or village could suffer the economic repercussions.

All three of the main heavy industries, mining, fishing and engineering, have

Whitby Abbey, a spectacular location on Yorkshire's east coast.

roots that go back at least to medieval times. Some of the richest coalfields were in South Yorkshire, and it is only within the last few decades that most of these mines have closed forever. Before the twentieth century, these coalfields provided fuel that was exported all over the world. Yorkshire's 114 miles of coast run along the east of the county and fishermen were braving the North Sea on a daily basis long before sonar equipment and expensive communication devices.

Those tracing an ancestor in one of these heavy industries have several excellent archives to rely on, to supplement traditional sources such as birth, marriage and death certificates. This chapter will look at some of the help available and what you can expect to find in these archives.

FISHING IN YORKSHIRE

Before the eighteenth century, fish was a foodstuff reserved only for the wealthy and those who lived within a short distance of the sea. The prohibitive cost of transporting fish inland before it decayed meant that seafood prices were out of reach of the budget of ordinary families.

However, as the eighteenth century progressed and urban populations continued to climb, masses of people needed to be fed at a low cost. This is when fish began to be used more widely as a cheap and plentiful food source and fishermen came to find their services in great demand.

Trawler boats had always operated in the south of England, particularly around Devon and the Thames area and many made a good living supplying fish for London markets. Gradually, the trawlermen came further around the coast away from the Thames area towards the North Sea. Some of the men would stay away from their home for the entire fishing season, living in local lodgings and fishing every day.

In 1821, two fishing smacks set out on a trawling venture sponsored by the

Hull Corporation and Colonel Ralph Creyke of Marton Hall. This was one of the first attempts to fish on a large scale off the coast of Yorkshire. Although the men's trawling gear was damaged during the trip, they felt that enough potential had come out of the expedition for it to be repeated.

The next few decades saw trawling take off in the East Yorkshire coastal areas. But when the trawlers landed at Scarborough to offload and sell their huge catches, they faced fierce opposition from local fisherman, jealous of their success and on several occasions were physically prevented from landing their catches in the town.

The trawlers moved to Hull, where they had a better reception and their fish was taken inland up the River Humber, eventually being particularly well received in Manchester. This was the first time that Manchester had received large consignments of fish to feed its population, which was growing hugely due to the jobs created by the Industrial Revolution.

The take off of the railways industry helped the fish trade to prosper, as for the first time perishable foodstuffs like

Maritime Museum, Hull.

fish could be transported quickly to the shops and markets where they were sold on. This stimulated the demand for trawlers and the lucrative trade brought in more fish than ever before. The years between 1840 and 1860 were particularly crucial in the growth of the trawling trade. This is shown by figures for the registration of fishing vessels in Hull. In 1840, there were seven fishing vessels registered in the town. Ten years later there were thirty-five, in 1860, the number had increased to 177 and by 1870 there were 250, with 400 just eight years later. It was estimated that, by 1883, the fish trade in Hull was worth over £1 million and employed over 2,000 people in the area.

Fishing had always been a trade that had passed from father to son, with families taking pride in being fishing folk in a particular area. Skippers often had a young apprentice living with them and taught them the trade from a young age. But as the trade grew so quickly, this efficient system began to deteriorate and the number of apprentices needed could no longer keep pace with the number of skippers willing and able to house them.

For the first time, in the mid-nineteenth century, fishing apprentices were taken in large numbers, from the age of 11 upwards, from institutions such as workhouses, charitable institutions and homeless shelters. The 'outdoor system' began to be operated on a large scale. This meant that, instead of living with a ship's skipper and his family, apprentices were expected to find their own board and lodgings when ashore. They were often drawn into drinking and gambling and desertions were common, an offence punishable by imprisonment.

There are several archives that offer the possibility of finding out more about ancestors who worked in the fishing trade. These are based mainly in the coastal areas of Yorkshire, but most welcome enquiries if you are unable to visit in person.

Hull Maritime Museum, Hull

This museum, in Hull's city centre, is housed in the city's former docks offices. It tells the story of Hull's maritime industry and how the industry built up from medieval times onwards. The city's maritime history is recounted through exhibits featuring ships and trawlers, models of boats and paintings. A section of the museum is devoted to the now outlawed pastime of whaling, which was once a major employer in Hull.

The museum has a small archive relating to some of the region's shipyards and shipbuilders. These include Cochranes shipyard archives from 1884 to 1995. The material held includes cash and wages books, minutes of directors' meetings, as well as records for Hull Shipbuilders Cook, Welton & Gemmel. These archives have details of all the vessels built by the company between 1883 and 1963.

Sailors' Families Society, Hull

The Sailors' Families Society at Hull is a registered charity which began in 1821 as a maritime charity. The fact that the society still helps families in need today speaks of how useful it has been to seafaring families down the generations.

The society has been caring for sailors' children since it was founded. Children might come under its care after the death of a seafaring relative, when a widow would have faced a bleak life without the wages of the main bread-winner. The society holds records on all of the children who have passed through its care.

In 1862, an orphan house was opened in Hull's Castle Row with the purpose of sheltering and educating those eligible for help. There was also an education programme for sea apprentices, who were taught the basics of reading, writing and arithmetic, as well as seafaring skills such as navigation, to equip them to make a living from the sea.

The society had a ship's library, opened on the floating chapel *Valiant* which operated from 1823 until the 1970s. The contents of the library give an idea of what sailors old and young would have read for leisure and to educate themselves.

In September 2005, the society made the decision to hand its complete archive to Hull City Archives. This will preserve the archives as the society moves from the premises it has occupied for a century.

The archives date back to the society's earliest days in 1821 and include copies of the society's magazine *Ashore and Afloat*, as well as committee records and information about the children who were helped by the society. Most of the files relating to the children can only be used by next of kin, or with per-mission from the society.

Whitby Museum

Whitby is one of the most famous fishing towns on the east coast. It has a long maritime history, including its association with Captain James Cook who was apprenticed to a Whitby ship owner in 1746.

The Whitby museum, located in the town centre, has an extensive archive, open by appointment, which covers most aspects of life in the town. The archives are strong on sailing and shipping and the collection includes more than thirty ships' logs, journals and account books, muster rolls of Whitby ships' crews 1708–1805 and 1835–8, and an eighteenth-century Protest Book, which recorded damage to ships.

There are over 10,000 volumes relating to the town of Whitby and its history and over 800 maps, including some of the earliest maps of the local area. Other aspects of community life represented in the archives include papers on the Whitby seamen's hospital (1753–1851) and poor relief accounts for 1774–1840.

SHIPBUILDING

For every person that sailed the seas, there were perhaps another twenty involved in shipbuilding and repairs. Hull was one of the main centres for these industries and this fact is reflected in the wealth of archives available in the city.

Hull University archives hold dozens of important business records, many of which relate to shipbuilding and maintenance. One of the collections held at the university archives relates to Earle's Shipbuilding and Engineering Co. Ltd, a Hull firm which employed up to 3,000 local men at the height of its prosperity. The firm was established in 1845 by brothers Charles and William Earle. Among the many ships built there were the famous Wilson Line vessels.

Although Earle's prospered in the golden age of ocean liners at the turn of the nineteenth century, by the depression years of the 1920s the shipyard was working on short time and many men were laid off, with the yard finally closing in 1932. Among the papers held by the archives relating to this firm are estimates of the cost of building many of the fine ships that Earle's produced, a list of the firm's shareholders and draft balance sheets.

The Ellerman Wilson Line company purchased Earle's shipbuilding during the 1890s when the firm entered voluntary liquidation. Earle's was allowed to keep its business name. This was only one of several firms owned by Ellerman's, who by the early twentieth century were the largest privately owned shipping company in the world, with over one hundred ships sailing the globe.

Like Earle's, Ellerman's suffered greatly in the depression of the 1920s and 1930s and, like many shipbuilders, lost business during the Second World War. They were never to recover fully and ceased trading in the 1970s.

Over 1,000 items relating to the company's history have been deposited at the university's archives. Items include bills of sale and mortgage for some of the company's ships, instructions and regulations for ship's officers, personnel details for masters and officers and a detailed family tree for the Wilson family. Items such as work instructions and regulations can give a great deal of information about life on board ship and how conditions and workload varied from rank to rank.

MINING

By its nature, coal mining was often an industry that kept few records of employees. Often, the work was on a casual basis, with men working as and when needed. Because of the high turnover of workers, few records of employees were kept. Also, the fact that many big mines have gone out of business means that their records were often lost or destroyed when the pits closed.

It is difficult to overstate how mining dominated the physical landscape of

South Yorkshire and hard to imagine the number of people whose livelihoods depended directly or indirectly on coal mining. We got used to hearing about mines closing down at the end of the twentieth century, but as late as 1950 the North Nottinghamshire and South Yorkshire coalfields were still employing around 40,000 men.

Accidents

The fact that the mining industry could be such a physically dangerous one meant that accidents in the pits were often reported in local newspapers and so recorded for posterity. Learning more about mining accidents through contemporary newspaper reports or coroner's records shows what working conditions were like at a particular time and the risks faced every day by employees.

One disaster at Cadeby colliery in 1912 had a particularly harsh impact on the whole local mining community because of the number of people killed in the incident. Two explosions at the colliery left 63 widows and 132 children without a father. The cruellest irony was that the second explosion, which killed 53 people, actually caused more fatalities than the original explosion, in which 35 had died. The victims of the second explosion had been going in to rescue those involved in the first blast. After the disaster, a relief fund was set up to pay out to the widows and children of those killed.

Local newspapers often reported upon disputes or closures at various pits, particularly in South Yorkshire, so it is always worth looking at local and even national newspapers around the time of troubles, to read their take on events. The Thornhill Mining disaster of July 1893 was a South Yorkshire pit disaster which touched the nation. Documents which remain from the tragedy illustrate how a local catastrophic event could end up affecting people who lived miles away from the area, and who had never been near a pit.

The disaster at the Thornhill pit killed 139, following an underground explosion, which only seven men survived. The disaster took place at a time of unrest in the mining industry; a national miners' strike had been planned for three weeks after the disaster. Although mining safety measures had been introduced, including the use of safety lamps, mining accidents such as that at Thornhill were common in the Yorkshire area.

After the disaster, the *Dewsbury Reporter* (which can be viewed at Huddersfield Local Studies Library) observed that there had been 29 Yorkshire colliery disasters since 1841. The paper listed these, including an accident at Oaks Colliery in 1866, Swaite Main in 1875 and Lundhill, Barnsley, in 1857.

The aftermath of the Thornhill disaster must have affected the neighbourhood heavily, with over 100 members of the community lost. The *Dewsbury Reporter* wrote that the village had many houses with curtains drawn out of respect for the dead and that 'in many cases, two or three houses together showed signs of the angel of death having visited the households'.

The town's parochial hall was used as a temporary morgue and relatives had the grim task of visiting the building to claim their relatives from the rows of dead. The burial register for the town's church, St Michael's, is at Wakefield archives, and 15 pages are given to entries for the deaths of the disaster victims. On the Saturday after the disaster, 91 funerals of victims were held.

A relief fund was set up for the families of the dead and this appeal touched the nation. The tragedy of the incident contrasted sharply with the celebrations the same week for the royal wedding of the future King George V and Queen Mary, which took place in London and was attended by Queen Victoria.

Donations to the relief fund flooded in from across the country. Kirklees archives holds original documents relating to the setting up and running of the fund. A cash account book at the archives shows the donations made by the public, including a collection from fans at a cricket match against Australia.

A booklet produced by the relief committee details each person or organization that gave a donation, including the amount donated. Pledges ranged from the 2s 6d given by 'an Edinburgh lad' to £100 from the Sowerby Bridge Flour Society and £200 from the Right Hon. Lord Savile. Individuals and groups who had nothing to do with mining donated to the cause, showing just how Thornhill had entered the consciousness of people across the country.

The mine's owner Edward Theodore Ingham is said to have broken down at the thought of what had happened as a result of the accident. The way in which local newspapers of the time reported Ingham's part in events after the incident shows that, despite what had happened, he was still held in good regard by the community. He seems to have been viewed as a fair employer.

A headline in the *Dewsbury Chronicler* (which can also be viewed at Huddersfield Local Studies Library) 'Colliery owner weeps at relief fund meeting' opened the lead article on 8 July about how Ingham had been received by relief fund committee members at their meeting. The story of how this employer had been affected by the accident is a good example of how many bosses saw their workers as an extension of their own family.

Edward Ingham had, he told the committee, made every effort to get back from Ireland as quickly as he could, being alarmed by the first telegram he received an hour after the event and subsequent messages, which confirmed how bad the situation at the pit had become.

Ingham told those at the meeting that, all the way home on the train, he felt as if he could hear the words 'widows and orphans' echoing in his head to the rhythm of the train. The newspaper claimed that Ingham was on first-name terms with most of his workers – 'they were like my own children', he told the committee.

The relief fund meeting closed with the members extending their sympathies for the accident to Ingham and once again underlining the fact that they did not find him to blame for the disaster. The chairman ended the meeting with rousing praise for his fellow Yorkshiremen, saying:

It makes a man proud of his countrymen to stand at the pithead in such circumstances as those of Tuesday evening, and to see them risking their lives for the sake of others . . . I have never felt so proud of Englishmen in my life before.

Strikes and closures

The *Yorkshire Post and Leeds Intelligencer* (which can be viewed at Leeds Local Studies Library) carried a report on 20 December 1880 about the temporary closure of the Denaby Main colliery near Doncaster and the laying off of workers. This must have come a particularly difficult time, just before Christmas. The newspaper reported that the owners had given their workmen notice to leave and that around 1,000 men and boys had been affected, which would have had a huge effect on the local economy, particularly in an area which depended heavily on the mining industries.

Most of the houses and properties in the Denaby Main area, including the Denaby Main hotel were owned by the Denaby Main colliery, which would have given the company great power over its employees and the local community. Despite the lay-offs of 1880, and others which followed, the colliery operated until 1968.

The newspaper reported that the colliery was the deepest in Yorkshire at 450 yards deep and that it had excellent transport facilities, being situated near a railway and canal. Coal mines depended upon good links with the outside world, so that the coal could be exported to the outside world quickly, thus bringing money into the business.

National Coal Mining Museum, Wakefield

The museum has been the country's national museum of coal mining since 1995 and holds a vast archive of items relevant to the industry. The coal mining museum is housed in a former pit, giving real authenticity to a visit and the chance to see what life would have been like for mining ancestors.

There are over 5,000 items in the museum's collection, with the second half of the twentieth century particularly well represented. The museum holds items which would have otherwise been discarded as pit after pit closed. Although many documents and artefacts that would have been of interest to historians have been lost forever following pit closures, this museum concentrates on preserving and making available the material which remains.

The museum's library, which is open to members of the public by appointment, holds hundreds of books and papers relating not just to coal mining itself, but to the impact of the industry on the wider community. Items directly related to pit life include accident reports, which detail the names of those involved in incidents and the type of incident, giving a flavour of the risks involved in coal mining and showing what could go wrong, from large disasters, such as the one examined in the previous section, to smaller incidents such as a person becoming trapped in a coal lift.

The museum's collection also includes a set of questions for exam papers which coal mine managers and under-managers would have had to pass. The questions reveal just how much knowledge of mining and pit life was required before anyone could progress to management level.

There are hundreds of photographs of mines and miners as well as artwork, poems and books produced by, or about, miners. A collection of union banners shows the different affiliations throughout the years and there are collections of newspapers such as the *Mining Journal* and the *Colliery Guardian*. Such publications contain valuable information on a particular period, with items such as job adverts giving details of pay and job specifications. Editorial pages include information about news in the mining communities which would have affected ancestors in the industry, such as strikes, recessions and redundancies.

The *Colliery Guardian* is one of the best starting points for anyone interested in researching most aspects of this industry. The journal began in 1858, when the coal industry was supplying the massive demand for fuel created by the Industrial Revolution. The museum's library has an almost complete run of issues from 1878.

There is an annual *Guide to Coalfields*, which charts the fortunes of pits in Yorkshire and further afield, registering when a particular mine closed, which would have had a huge impact on the community that lived alongside that place of work. When a large number of men were out of work at once, local shops and business would have felt the effects as well, with everyone in the community losing money at once.

Another fascinating source available at the museum are the Inspector's Reports, which were instigated after the 1850 Act for the Inspection of Coal Mines in Great Britain. The reports vary in the amount of detail about accidents and who was involved and are particularly lacking in information during the First and Second World War periods. Nevertheless, they often give names of those killed in incidents and statistics about how an accident was dealt with and how rescue attempts were carried out.

MACHINERY AND ENGINEERING

Engineering was an important industry in the region, with many of the country's finest engineers coming from Yorkshire. Men such as Edmund Cartwright and Samuel Cunliffe Lister revolutionized the way thousands of people worked, through inventions which changed industries forever.

Edmund Cartwright, after whom Bradford's Cartwright Hall is named, invented the power loom which changed weaving from a home-based, small-scale process operated by outworkers, to a large-scale factory-based industry.

Cartwright was born in Nottinghamshire in 1743, and built his first weaving shed in Yorkshire, at Doncaster. His patented power loom did not bring him personal success, but it transformed the weaving industry.

Samuel Cunliffe Lister's contribution to machinery invention in the nineteenth century was to produce a wool-combing machine that was so efficient it caused a large drop in the price of clothing as a direct result of its effectiveness. He also created a silk-combing machine that utilized hitherto unusable silk waste. Both men could claim that their personal talents had improved and modernized the textile trade noticeably.

Such achievements were not always popular with those who had made their living as outworkers, producing textiles at home. Such advances in the textile trade were partly to blame for the outbreaks of violence attributed to the Luddites around the years 1811–17. During this period, mobs of disgruntled workers attacked mills, smashing the machines they blamed for the loss of their livelihood.

Local newspapers of the time reported on events such as an attack on Rawfolds Mill near Brighouse in April 1812. This outbreak of violence led to the murder of a mill owner a few days later and 17 men were sentenced to death following the incidents. Machine breaking became a capital offence following the Frame Breaking Act of 1812. However, the fact that the violence continued shows how serious workers felt the issue was.

Most areas of Yorkshire have been able to boast engineering trades, and there were also several spin-off industries. Mill towns such as Halifax and Bradford had strong industries working to provide the region's factories and mills with machinery and associated parts. Keighley was particularly noted for producing textile machinery and the spare parts needed as replacements.

Yorkshire Air Museum

Yorkshire has a strong engineering tradition in the field of aviation and, particularly during the First and Second World Wars, engineering skills were needed more than ever, to produce the planes that helped Britain to defeat her enemies. Perhaps Yorkshire's most famous female engineer is Amy Johnson, born in Hull in 1903. She was the first British-trained female ground engineer and paved the way for other women to enter a predominantly male industry.

The Yorkshire Air Museum is devoted to such air pioneers and to the planes they made and flew. If your ancestor was involved in aircraft production or flew planes, before, during or after the world wars, you will find plenty of information about the type of work in which they would have been involved. The museum houses an extensive aviation library which contains photographs and historical documents for RAF, RAAF and RCAF squadrons who served in the county. The Yorkshire Air Museum is discussed further in Chapter 8, in its capacity as a research centre for life during wartime.

STEEL

Steel is perhaps Yorkshire's most famous 'heavy' industry, conjuring up images of the huge chimneys and large cutlery factories that made up the landscape of South Yorkshire from Victorian times onwards.

The steel industry has traditionally centred around the city of Sheffield, which could boast connections with the trade from medieval times onwards. The town showed a boom in population during the Industrial Revolution, as people entered Sheffield from around Yorkshire and further afield to take advantage of the number of jobs available as steel making, railways and engineering all created employment. This boom is demonstrated by population figures for Sheffield in 1736 standing at 14,500 and then rising almost tenfold to over 135,000 by 1851.

One name synonymous with the steel trade and a man whose work helped to make the town famous for steel was Benjamin Huntsman, born in Lincolnshire in 1704. Huntsman made a big improvement to the steel industry through the use of a crucible in the metal's production process. He actually left Sheffield for France before the process was fully in use, because the cutlers of Sheffield would not work with his steel, saying it was too hard. While he was out of the country, his ideas were copied, steel improved and the industry as a whole prospered.

Huntsman eventually returned to the city and set up his steel works at Attercliffe in the Don Valley. This became one of the main locations for steel production in the city.

Sheffield Archives

The Sheffield Archives are one of the best places to find out more about what it was like to be a steel worker. The records of many steel firms came to be deposited with the archives when many firms amalgamated or closed during the second half of the twentieth century. These include business records for Joseph Elliot & Sons for 1835–1991, C G Carlisle & Co. Ltd (1920–70) and Edgar Allen & Co (1903–56).

The archives also hold a run of *The Bombshell*, a monthly works journal which was produced 'for the interests of the employees of Thomas Firth & Sons Ltd, Norfolk Works, Sheffield'. Magazines produced by firms such as Firth's can help to give a real understanding of the work culture and atmosphere at the company where an ancestor worked. The tone of the publication, the type of articles and the amount of information given about events and employees help build up a picture of what it would have been like to have worked there.

Thomas Firth & Sons began trading from Sheffield's Norfolk Works in 1842 and with John Browns (who they later amalgamated with) were responsible for some of the landmark breakthroughs in the steel industry during the nineteenth and twentieth centuries. These included the invention of stainless steel

Sheffield archives.

in 1913 and the use of the Bessemer process in 1860, which revolutionized the way steel was produced in Sheffield. In 1982, the amalgamated Firth Browns combined with the British Steel Corporation to form Sheffield Forgemasters, who still operate today.

The Bombshell is an A5 sized illustrated magazine, full of information about life at Thomas Firth's. It covers all aspects of life there; from working in the engineering department to serving in the canteen and offers many insights into both the lives of individual workers and into the facilities provided by the firm.

Sheffield archives hold a run of the magazine from 1921 to 1926 and, from the editorial section at the beginning of each issue, it is clear that the 1920s were a difficult time for manufacturers throughout the city and the country as a whole. Several times, one of the firm's managing directors appealed through the magazine's pages, alongside a photograph of himself, for workers not to lose hope and to pull together, at one point stating that 'bickering and strife are of no value at this juncture'.

The magazines are not all gloomy though. *The Bombshell* is a lively read, and looking through the different items is almost like having an informal chat with one of the firm's workers. The 'we should like to know' section is particularly amusing, and is full of gossip about various topics of debate around the company. The items include questions such as 'who won the wrist watch that was raffled off in the sheet mills?' and 'is it possible for the Yorkshire pudding at the Savile Street Canteen to get any thinner?' It is trivial, light-hearted information like this which brings to life our picture of the day-to-day existence of our ancestors.

Thomas Firth's seem to have employed adults of all ages, a fact which can be seen through the range of articles published, with something to interest almost everyone. Features included a regular mystery story, articles on travel and hobbies and book reviews, covering recent releases. The books reviewed ranged from light fiction reads to more serious tomes and one suggestion was the book *300 Things a Bright Boy Can Do*. Priced at 7s 6d, the book's editor stated that 'too many youths fall into mere aimless dawdling'. The magazine suggested that the book would be an ideal gift for a young male relative, giving them ideas about hobbies and interests.

The Bombshell is illustrated throughout with photographs and cartoons. The photographs are particularly valuable to anyone tracing an ancestor who worked here during the 1920s, as many of the group photographs, and all of the single shots, include names. Most of the issues focused one or two employees, with a short biography of the person and details of their life at work and home. Anyone who has an ancestor featured in this section would consider themselves very lucky indeed, because of the amount of information which was given. A 1921 issue features Phil Pitcher who joined the firm in 1888 and since then had 'steadfastly refused to sample any inferior firms'.

Firth's seem to have been particularly proud of those who provided the firm with long service. The firm entered its long-standing employees for a contest organized by the *Sheffield Daily Independent*, titled 'faithful old hands of industry'. Despite the Firth's team having an aggregate age of 302.5 years, they were beaten by John Brown's, who could boast an employee who had been at their Atlas works for an incredible 69 years.

The magazine is full of information about the out-of-hours activities organized by the company, which included a women's hockey team, bowls, billiards, tennis and rifle clubs. Outings to places such as Scarborough and the Lake District are also mentioned. Finally, another out-of-hours activity was the Christmas party organized by Firth's and described in a 1926 issue of *The Bombshell*. It makes fascinating reading, as it is difficult to imagine such a civilized, restrained event taking place at a twenty-first-century workplace. According to the magazine, the party began with a pianoforte solo by a Miss M Stacey, and was followed by songs and cello music. The proceedings were rounded off with Miss Stacey and her fellow performers being presented with boxes of chocolates and applauded by the party-goers. What hardened steel workers made of the genteel celebrations is something we can only guess at!

Kelham Island Museum

This is a popular industrial museum with collections relating to Sheffield's industrial past. Many people, however, are unaware that the museum also holds a huge collection of artefacts and archives which are available to researchers who make an appointment.

The museum stands in the city's industrial quarter, on a man-made island which is over 900 years old. The museum itself holds hundreds of artefacts about how Sheffield developed as an industrial main-player and the people and industries which made the city so successful. A visit makes an ideal starting point for finding out about industries in which your ancestor might have been involved.

Behind the scenes, though, is where the real research material lies. The museum houses the majority of historic collections held by the Sheffield Industrial Museums Trust, which date from the 1750s. There is a research facility for members of the public who wish to have access to the collections by prior appointment.

All of Sheffield's major industries are represented in the collections, including iron and steel making, cutlery and tool making, and mechanical and electrical engineering. Artefacts in the archives include machinery and tools used in the various industrial processes, as well as items used by workers, such as safety clothing and health and safety items.

One of the most important collections is that of the personal papers of Harry Brearley, the man who invented stainless steel. There are also actual examples of the steel he worked on to perfect the product which was one of Sheffield's major exports. The museums holds a collection of film recordings and over 50,000 photographs which have been donated by various Sheffield companies and which relate to industrial manufacturing processes and the products which were created via these processes.

RAILWAYS

Like the rest of England, Yorkshire benefited hugely from the arrival of railways in the region during the nineteenth century. Because of the huge amount of manpower needed to cut railway lines throughout the county, many of us will have had an ancestor who was involved with the railway industry.

When railways reached cities, towns and villages, whole communities suddenly had access to areas that had previously been impracticable to reach. People were able to move around more easily, meaning that they could migrate to different areas where work was plentiful.

During the mid-nineteenth century, large sections of many communities were involved in helping the railway industry to expand. One such instance was 'the plant' in Doncaster: in 1853, the Great Northern Railway Co. opened a locomotive works there, which came to be known as 'the plant'. This became a major employer in the town and many of its records were donated to the National Railway Museum at York. Doncaster archives hold a record of everyone employed at the plant from 1887 onwards, and a register of workers employed there between 1897 and 1948.

Although railways brought great prosperity to some, there were inevitably some tragedies, involving rail workers or train travellers. Local newspapers carried details about rail accidents, which often went into great detail about the accident, the circumstances surrounding it, the rescue operation and details of those killed or injured.

A report in the *Yorkshire Post* of 22 December 1880 gives an example of what sort of information could be reported. The article reports that one person had been killed and forty injured in a rail collision outside Leeds railway station. The collision had been between two trains, one bound for Bristol and the other for Sheffield. According to the *Yorkshire Post*, the Sheffield train had gone onto the wrong track and had collided with the other train which was coming from the opposite direction.

The paper reported that, after the accident, word spread quickly around Leeds and such a big crowd gathered to watch the rescue operation that the officials were not able to go about their work until the people had been moved on. Bonfires were lit at the side of the tracks, to aid the rescuers and men with torches were sent out from the station. A Mrs Southall of Park Row, Normanton Common, died in the incident and her husband suffered two broken legs. The paper goes on to give the names of the others injured in the accident, with details of the injuries sustained.

National Railway Museum, York

The archives of the National Railway Museum in York have built up, since the railway museum's opening in 1975, into one of the largest collections of railway books, maps, photographs and archives in the country. There are over 20,000 books and 1.4 million photographs in the collections, which include information on British railway history, and also railway accidents and information about the construction of railways in Yorkshire and other areas.

Also available to consult are maps of railway companies, a timetable collection, copies of official railway accident reports from 1855 onwards and engineering drawings, as well as papers by notable people in the railway industry and the archives of railway workers' associations.

CONFECTIONERY

One of Yorkshire's most appealing industries is that of confectionery production, something which has featured in the county's towns and villages since medieval times. Some of the country's most famous sweet products were manufactured in Yorkshire by Terrys and Rowntrees of York.

Pontefract produced some of Yorkshire's finest confectionery.

Rowntrees of York

Papers held at the Borthwick Institute of Historical Research, York, relate, often in great detail, what life was like working for one of the most famous and successful confectionery manufacturers in the world.

The Rowntrees family employed thousands of York people at their chocolate works and they prided themselves on personal contact with their employees. The various roles open to workers can be seen in the records of directors' meetings. These included work in the company's pension and welfare departments, in the medical section or on the factory floor. One of the most unusual departments to work in was the West Indian section. This was concerned with administering the overseas estates owned by Rowntrees during the nineteenth century, for the purpose of growing cocoa.

Records concerning the administrative history of Rowntrees at the Borthwick Institute detail how staff were cared for in a company that was seen as being ahead of its time in terms of employee welfare. Among the benefits available to Rowntrees' workers during the twentieth century were a works canteen, pension and welfare funds and a company policy to 'care for the well-being of employees in all respects conducive to their efficiency as workers and to their development as individuals'.

Of particular interest to anyone trying to trace an ancestor who worked at the company before or during the First World War are the company's staff office papers. These were compiled to comply with civil defence requirements and list every male member of staff from age 16 to 41, giving their name, age, marital status, job title and any relevant military exemption.

Office staff record books, which relate to the first decades of the twentieth century, go into even more detail. These list employee's name, address, name of father, education, previous employment, departments worked in at Rowntrees and the quality of their work at the company. Even more interesting are records of any events of significance at home, such as births or deaths and also the reason the person left Rowntrees, if applicable.

Rowntrees were one of the first companies to introduce a paid week's holiday in 1918, decades before other businesses followed their example, and the company also provided a doctor and dentist. Rowntrees' magazine, *The Cocoa Works*, provided bulletins on everyday life and different developments at the chocolate factory.

Working conditions at Rowntrees were the envy of many other companies and finding out more about the benefits the company offered is a fascinating insight into how things could be done well and what day-to-day life would have been like for an ancestor who worked one of the world's most famous confectionery firms.

Chapter 2

FROM SERGES TO SARIS: THE TEXTILE TRADE

From the nineteenth century onwards, Yorkshire was known throughout the world as a top-class producer of textiles. Richly hued velvets, soft tweeds, feather-light saris and heavy brocades were just some of the materials produced in the county's towns and cities.

Yorkshire has been a producer of textiles since at least medieval times. Bridges such as this one at Ilkley allowed wool traders to move between communities.

Many Yorkshire communities made their fortune from wool.

Many of these settlements had dozens of mill chimneys on their skylines and their streets echoed to the sound of clogged workers making their way to and from the mill and to the noise of hundreds of looms working to produce cloth around the clock. Although machines could produce materials much quicker than anyone working from home could have ever achieved, workers were still needed to man the looms. Many mills only closed on Sundays and mill employees worked various shifts to cover the hours needed.

Yorkshire's landscape made it a prime producer of textiles from medieval times onwards. Plentiful access to soft water, naturally filtered through layers of peat, miles of open moorland for sheep to graze and entrepreneurs willing to grow their textile businesses in the county's towns combined to make Yorkshire one of the country's biggest producers of quality textiles, for use at home and all over the world.

Yorkshire really came into its own as a producer of textiles during the Industrial Revolution when a series of inventions turned several of the county's towns from insignificant hamlets into thriving cities, with thousands of inhabitants arriving every year to take up jobs in textile mills. This is why so many people who would not otherwise have been connected to the county have Yorkshire ancestors. Word spread around England that there were plenty of mill jobs in the area, particularly in the West Riding, and many families uprooted themselves from places where they had been settled for generations in order to begin new lives working in Yorkshire textiles.

Towns such as Bradford and Huddersfield were ill equipped to deal with the sudden influx of immigrants arriving from the rest of the UK and overseas. Although people were aware that there were jobs aplenty in the region's mills, towns that were used to having small populations suddenly found themselves housing thousands of extra people, young and old.

Some of the records we will explore in this chapter shed light on the consequences of sudden population influxes. Industrial accidents, reports of slum dwelling and terrible overcrowding were just some of the results of the industrial boom in textile towns. Newspaper, coroners' reports, accident books and factory inspection records build up a picture of the sometimes appalling living and working conditions our ancestors had to endure.

THE WEST RIDING TEXTILE INDUSTRIES

The city of Bradford is a prime example of what could happen when too many people crowded into a town over a short period of time. In 1801, the town had just over 6,300 inhabitants, compared to its neighbour Leeds which could boast almost ten times as many people. Just 50 years later, the population of Bradford had grown by almost 30 times, standing at 182,000 Graveyards were overcrowded, people were forced to share toilets, houses and sometimes even bedrooms with other families and the average life expectancy was just over 18 years.

Despite these startling figures of unprecedented growth, the textile trade did provide many people with a good and steady living. As well as the thousands of people who worked on the mill floor, there were men who made their fortunes from the textile industry and who provided employment for the ordinary workers.

Documents held at Bradford's archives, relating to Drummond's, one of the city's biggest textile employers, give a good idea of what mill life was like. A brochure produced to celebrate the British Empire Exhibition of 1924 tells prospective customers how good it was to work for Drummond's. Although the brochure is very enjoyable to read, with its illustrations of various workers and workplaces, it is important to remember that it was produced to give a good impression of the firm to existing and potential clients and so the information given is somewhat biased. Nevertheless, it is an excellent primary source for mill life in the city.

Most textile mills were governed by the buzzer, which could often be heard streets away and which summoned workers to the beginning of the working day. No one was allowed to go for a break or leave for the day until the buzzer had sounded. The Drummond's brochure states that workers at some factories wasted time in chatting to each other and so missed vital working minutes

The homes occupied by textile barons were often in stark contrast to the living conditions of their workers (Cliffe Castle, Keighley).

simply because they did not realize what the time was. Drummond's, stated the pamphlet proudly, benefited from an electrically synchronized system of 36 clocks, so that no employee could use the excuse that they were unaware of the time.

The brochure also features a photograph of long-serving employees, with each one named, together with their length of service. Many textile workplaces would present a long-serving employee with a present upon retirement, or at a landmark anniversary such as 30 years of service. Such events were often featured in company magazines and even local newspapers, so if you suspect one of your ancestors remained in one job for a good while, it is worth checking company records and newspapers around the time a landmark anniversary or retirement would have occurred.

PHILANTHROPISTS

Many nineteenth-century textile mill owners have been accused of putting profits before the welfare of their employees, but there were some who could provide proof that a mill could make a decent profit and still treat its staff well. On this theme, the Kirklees office of West Yorkshire archive service holds material on Colonel Edward Akroyd who was responsible for creating a model village for his workers, with on-site amenities such as a library and school. This community was run along similar lines to Titus Salt's model village Saltaire, which also features in this chapter.

Akroyd encouraged thrift among his employees by establishing a penny savings bank, which has now become the high street Yorkshire Bank. The archives hold an 1857 Huddersfield election poster which describes how well the mill owner treated his workers. It is a superb example of Victorian paternalism and, in attempting to make out Edward Akroyd to be a worthy election candidate, the poster invites all prospective voters to visit any of Akroyd's establishments and see for themselves the excellent treatment his employees received.

The poster states that Akroyd employed more than 5,000 people and at Copley village there was a day school for 600 children. Akroyd provided a band for his workers' amusement, which played on summer evenings at the recreation ground. At his Haley Hill site there was a medical dispensary, a clothing society and garden allotments, which the mill owner donated as prizes to workers.

'These things are not paraded for the purpose of gaining your vote for Mr Akroyd', stated the poster. 'His conduct as an employer is the expression of his sense of duty towards the men, women and children, whose industrial chief he is.' Despite the fact that this poster is clearly canvassing for votes, it does an excellent job of outlining what was important to the Victorian public and what a person had to do to be considered a good employer. The facilities provided by Akroyd were better than most mill employees working in an inner-city factory could expect, but they did exist and anyone living in one of Akroyd's villages could make use of them.

THE NORTH RIDING LINEN INDUSTRY

As we have seen, the vast majority of historical records relating to the textile industry concern the old West Riding area, and particularly the area which makes up modern West Yorkshire, including Leeds, Bradford, Halifax and Huddersfield. However, there was a thriving linen industry in the North Riding, and records exist from the eighteenth century onwards. Many of these are held at the North Yorkshire County Record Office at Northallerton.

Textiles was not such a major employer in the North Riding as it became in the West Riding, partly because the northern areas of the county were made up of small, dispersed towns and villages, making it difficult to gather a large workforce. Also the area did not benefit as much from the plentiful access to fuel and water power that made the West Riding area such a success.

Although some flax was grown locally in the southern vale of York and Ryedale, most of the raw material for the area's linen making came from Holland and the Baltic. Port books for Hull and Whitby show that, during the eighteenth century, there was a huge increase in the amount of flax being imported, indicating a healthy demand for the raw material. The port of Hull imported just over 1,700 cwts of flax in 1702, which had increased dramatically to over 45,000 cwts by 1783. Similarly, Whitby imported over 1,900 cwts of flax in 1790 and 4,060 cwts, just ten years later.

The linen industry in the area suffered a depression during the 1820s, when rioting was reported in Knaresborough as a result of low employment in the trade. However, the 1831 census for the North Riding still showed over 300 weavers living in the area. Textiles in the North Riding were slower to mechanize than in the West Riding, perhaps because the communities were more scattered and so developments were slower to spread. Also, the North Riding, with its small country villages, could not accommodate huge numbers of migrants in the way that larger already established urban population centres such as Leeds and Bradford did.

The *Yorkshire Gazette*, in April 1841, reported that wages of weavers in the North Riding were 'low and uncertain' and that they were 'out of work a third of their time'. This is in contrast to the boom in the textile trade following the Industrial Revolution in Leeds and Bradford, where hundreds of mills employed thousands of workers and mills such as Lister's and Salt's were amongst the biggest in the world. The working and living conditions of those residing in West Yorkshire may have been less desirable than those of their rural North Yorkshire counterparts, but most people who wanted a job in the textile industry in West Yorkshire could find one.

Knaresborough seems an idyllic Yorkshire town but was once the scene of textile riots.

It could be harder to find work in isolated rural areas (Horton in Ribblesdale).

By the time of the 1851 census, figures for the North Riding area showed that, in contrast to the burgeoning textile centres of the West Riding, many of those who had worked in the area as weavers had migrated overseas, particularly to America. The abstract of census returns reported that:

> The decrease of population in various places in the Northallerton district is ascribed to depression in the linen trade which has caused emigration beyond the seas and the removal of many families to more prosperous localities.

Census returns for the principal North Riding linen weaving townships over the period 1801–51 show in most cases that many families had been forced to leave their home towns because the area's principal industry, i.e. linen, could no longer offer them work. Thornton le Dale began the nineteenth century in 1801 with 731 inhabitants, which had risen to 937 just thirty years later. But by the 1851 census there were only 796 inhabitants remaining. Similarly, Osmotherley had 534 inhabitants in 1801, rising to 1,087 in 1831 and falling to 935 in 1851.

The clear contrast in the fortunes of the North and West Riding textile industries is an interesting illustration of how the geography of an area could have an effect on its fortunes. While people were moving into the West Riding at a great rate when the textile industry was at its height during the nineteenth century, North Riding textile workers were being forced out of the area and overseas due to the poor performance of their industry.

The fluctuations of the textile trade, particularly during the nineteenth century, could be a clue as to why ancestors sometimes disappear from records between censuses. Contemporary newspaper reports may give information about the closure of mills which could have affected whole communities, causing families to uproot and move to an area where they could hope to find work. In an age before unemployment benefits, loyalty to a home town often had to come after the need to find a job in order to survive.

TEXTILE ARCHIVES

Yorkshire, as befitting a county with such a rich textile heritage, has a number of excellent archive repositories which contain material relating to the area's textile industry. All of the local record offices in the county hold information relating to the mills in their own areas.

Such records can include accident books, financial details, visitor books, wage books and employee records. Although items like wage books and accounts sound like an excellent way of finding an ancestor who worked in textiles, it is actually quite rare to find employees named in such records.

There are of course exceptions, such as the Drummond's brochure mentioned earlier in the chapter, where individual employees are named and pictured. However, if you decide to research the industry as a whole, or just a

Mills and factories employed whole communities.

particular firm where an ancestor worked, there is plenty you can find to give background information about life in textiles, with the outside chance that you may find an individual ancestor named as a bonus.

The Colour Museum

Bradford's Colour Museum is the only museum of colour in the UK. It houses the archives of the Society of Dyers and Colourists, which was founded in 1884. Bradford gained a fine reputation for the quality and colourfastness of its dyeing work early in its textile history.

Unless your ancestor was a member of the Society of Dyers and Colourists you would be unlikely to find details of a particular person in the archives. What you will find, though, is plenty of information about the various companies that dyed cloth and yarn in West Yorkshire and beyond. Items such as factory rules, which prohibited smoking and fined latecomers, are testament to a way of life which has now largely disappeared with the closure of most of the county's textile mills.

Factories like the Bradford-based Ripley's dye works specialized in supplying colourfast black garments, which were immensely popular with the working classes and so sold widely. The Society of Dyers and Colourists, which still exists today, is a professional body dedicated to preserving and furthering the science of colour.

Stainless steel printing roller – many textile patterns were detailed and intricate (courtesy of the Colour Museum, Bradford).

Medieval dyeing: dyeing is one of the oldest trades in the country (courtesy of the Colour Museum, Bradford).

There are two main areas to the archives at the Colour Museum. The first is dedicated to artefacts that were used in the dyeing and printing of fabrics. These give a fascinating idea of how the trade has changed over the years. For example, a printing block designed to be pressed on to a fabric often had immensely fine detail and had to be used with skill and precision. Other items such as dyer's notebooks, accidentally stained with the colours used in dyeing materials to the required shade, can be seen to have been used regularly by the amount of wear and tear they show.

If your ancestor was a member of the Society of Dyers and Colourists, there is a good chance you will find reference to them in the extensive holdings of the second half of the archives at the museum. This section contains hundreds of written documents ranging from wartime service military exemption certificates for certain staff working in mills, to dinner menus and photographs of those who attended the society's annual celebrations. Several prominent families from the area have donated documents and papers.

The collection also includes items from large textile mills which carried out dyeing as only one part of the whole textile creation process. These include mills such as Lister's, a mill which could produce a piece of fabric from start to finish, rather than specializing in one part of the process, such as weaving, as did many mills. Lister's had its own separate dyehouse, so that the finished fabric did not have to be sent anywhere else after production, but could be shipped out straight from the mill.

Lister's mill had its own company magazine and copies are held at the Colour Museum archives. Various types of events, from news of staff marriages and retirements, to reports of social events and new initiatives at the mill, paint a detailed picture of what life was like working for one of Europe's largest mills. The colour museum archives also hold every copy of the journal of the Society of Dyers and Colourists, which has been produced continuously since 1885.

Saltaire Studies Centre

Staying in West Yorkshire, the most famous part of the county for textiles, we will explore the holdings of the Saltaire Studies Centre. This is a little-known archive that is part of Shipley College. Anyone familiar with the history of West Yorkshire is likely to have heard of the town of Saltaire and its founder Titus Salt.

Titus Salt was a wealthy mill owner who created a model village for his workers to take them away from the stench and poverty of inner-city Bradford. He was a mill employee at one of the lowest points in Bradford's history, when poverty and disease were so rife that many people never reached adulthood.

Salt has been criticized for being over-paternalistic and too controlling of his workforce, but he built Saltaire at a stage in his life when he was rich enough to retire from textiles and live out the rest of his life in luxury. Instead of retiring, Salt created a village that took the rest of his days to finish. He worked longer hours than many of his employees and created a place to live and work that was far superior to anything on offer in nearby Bradford.

Whatever anyone's opinion on Titus Salt, a visit to the Saltaire Studies Centre is a

Titus Salt, one of Yorkshire's most famous industrialists.

Salt's mill, the centrepiece of the model village Saltaire.

chance to find out what life was like for people who lived and worked in Saltaire or similar model villages. The archive is made up of various items relating to the town of Saltaire and to the Salt family. The archives for the town include Ordnance Survey plans of Saltaire and nearby Shipley, as well as various plans for the conversion or extension of various buildings in Saltaire at different points in the town's history. There are plans to convert houses into shops and material relating to the extension of one of the mill's wool warehouses and the combing mill. There is an extensive collection of photographs featuring local people, street scenes and pupils of Salt Grammar school.

The archives pertaining to the Salt family are a mixture of papers and artefacts. The Saltaire Studies Centre holds paperwork and correspondence relating to a royal visit to the town in 1887. As well as documents about the arrangements made and the visit itself, there are menu cards from the event and a signed photograph of Princess Beatrice.

There are also important items that belonged to the Salt family. Included in the collections are Titus Salt's cheque book and birth, marriage and death certificates for Titus Salt junior. A copy of Salt's will is also available to view. Although Salt amassed a huge fortune through the textile industry, he gave

Man cutting a hand printing block – just one of the hundreds of tasks associated with the textile industry (courtesy of the Colour Museum, Bradford).

away much of his fortune to charity and left only a few thousand pounds to those members of his family who survived him. He is buried in the Salt family mausoleum beside the Saltaire Congregational Church.

Further items about Titus Salt are held at Bradford archives. The items housed there include directors' reports, visitor books, promotional literature and photographs from King George VI's visit to Saltaire in 1937. There are papers about the Salt family dating from 1861 to 1981 and information about the huge Milner Field Estate at Bingley, which was once the palatial home of Salt's son Titus Salt junior. The Milner Field mansion was the envy of people for miles around and included a dairy farm, riding stables and separate buildings for servants.

The Bradford Textile Archive

This is a relatively new archive, opened in 2000, which is part of the University of Bradford. The archive is open to the public but there are charges to use the facilities, and these are explained on the archive's website (www.textilearchive.bilk.ac.uk). The Bradford Textile Archive holds over one million textiles from all over the world and the records held include examples of experiments undertaken by Bradford College students from the 1890s onwards.

Bradford's success in the textile industry came partly because of its willingness to experiment with different types of yarn and combinations of materials. Tutors at the Bradford College encouraged their students to try new combinations of fabrics and different production techniques in the quest to produce the best cloth in the country. Tutors and students took their inspiration from all

Saltaire boasted many fine public buildings.

around the world, as reflected in the diversity of the cloth produced.

Of particular interest is the India Collection, which includes ethnic fabrics woven with gold thread and embellished with real beetle wings. The material available to examine here would give you a good idea of the type of cloth that your ancestor might have produced and the various production processes in which they would have been involved.

City of Bradford Technical College

Bradford was acknowledged as one of the world leaders in textiles from the nineteenth century, right through to the post-Second World War period when Bradford's mills began to lose trade to overseas markets which could produce cloth cheaper and faster. We have already read that the city's mills employed thousands of people, many of whom came from far afield to take up textile jobs. For most, the skills required for spinning or weaving were something that could be picked up in a few weeks after working alongside an experienced person.

However, other areas of textile production were much more specialized and required certain skills, some of which could only be taught away from the workplace. Work such as being an overlooker (a mill floor supervisor) or a textile designer required not just on-the-job training but after-hours teaching as well. Most of those who entered these trades did so straight from school, on the understanding that they were sent out from work to college on day release, or would be expected to give up their own free time and attend classes in the evenings. The level of commitment required was often considerable, with trainee overlookers attending college three nights a week throughout term times.

The City of Bradford Technical College was the most popular textile training institution in the area. It taught a range of classes relating to the textile industry and regularly held awards evenings where prizes were given to those who had given outstanding performances in their studies. The school was opened in 1882, at the height of Bradford's predominance as a global producer of textiles. There were four departments: textiles, art and design, engineering and chemistry and dyeing. The main college archives are at the J B Priestley library, at the University of Bradford.

The West Yorkshire Archives Bradford branch holds lecture notes for colour lectures, taken by Bradford College tutor George Senior in 1910. Senior's detailed notes and drawings illustrate just how much attention to detail and technical knowledge was required by anyone learning about how textiles were produced as part of their course of studies.

Alongside Senior's handwritten course notes are detailed sketches of textile patterns in various colours. The colours which are painted on the pages are shown in different combinations to illustrate to students how placing one colour next to another could totally alter the effect of a piece of fabric.

In his lecture notes, Senior stated that he believed there were both physical and physiological sides to how colours affected a person's eyes. He gave examples of how different colours could make people feel, with red being warm and cheerful, yellow bright and pure, and green cold and reserved. It is an inside account of how much thought went into the creation of fabrics before they even reached the weaving loom.

TEXTILE ACCIDENTS

Nineteenth-century mill workers took for granted working conditions that we would these days find intolerable. Accidents were an everyday part of life and there was little legislation to protect workers. Although philanthropists such as William Edward Forster (who introduced the 1870 Education Act) tried to improve working conditions for both children and adults, a lack of formal health and safety regulations meant that employees risked themselves working alongside potentially dangerous machinery on a daily basis.

A large-scale accident, such as Bradford's Newland's Mill disaster of 1882 would attract widespread media coverage. The accident, which is to date the city's worst industrial disaster, led to 54 deaths and nearly as many injuries. Local press coverage of the accident and its aftermath and documents relating to the inquest give a vivid picture of how an accident could affect a whole community, bringing all classes together and involving dozens of local people who did not even work at the mill.

The mill disaster has traditionally been blamed on the greed of its Victorian mill owner, Sir Henry Ripley, who commissioned a 255 foot high chimney for his textile mill at West Bowling in 1862. Ripley ignored the advice of his builders, determined to have the highest chimney in the area, a decision which was eventually to cost many of his workers their lives.

The fact that the chimney had to be propped up several times in the decades following its creation, and was often seen to blow in the wind, should have warned the mill owner that something was wrong. The 4,000 ton chimney collapsed on the morning of 28 December 1882, after a stormy night. Those killed by the falling masonry were mostly women and children who had been working in the mill complex. Local people, both police officers and volunteer members of the public, helped in the aftermath of the accident and many of those who took part in the rescue attempts are mentioned in press reports.

The town's local paper, the *Bradford Daily Telegraph*, carried daily reports giving great detail about those who had died, the progress and extent of the injuries of those fortunate enough to survive and, later, the results of the inquest, which took place on 9 January 1883. The inquest jury members came from all sections of society, their trades including a draper, innkeeper, quarry owner, coach builder and lithographer. The verdict reached was one of accidental death, despite the fact that the mill owners clearly knew of the danger of the perilous chimney. To our modern eyes, such a verdict may seem unfair, but it perhaps illustrates the lack of rules and regulations to protect workers at the time. Employee health and safety were not paramount concerns and most legislation existed to protect the employer rather than employees.

The case was taken to court privately a year later in 1884, by a James Henderson who had lost two teenage daughters in the accident. Again, it was reported that the judge decided strong winds had contributed to the fall of the chimney and a verdict of accidental death was awarded. The Ripley firm paid Henderson seven weeks' wages in compensation after the accident and the girls' funeral expenses. Henderson was left with five other younger children to support.

The site of the accident is marked by a plaque, naming the victims of the Newland's Mill tragedy. It was erected in 2002 on the 120th anniversary of the incident.

Chapter 3

GREAT ESTATES: LIVING AND WORKING ON THE LAND

The county's stately homes allowed privileged people to show their wealth and taste through their opulence of their houses and the amount of land they owned. The estates attached to the region's stately homes, such as Harewood House near Leeds, often covered hundreds of acres of land and employed many local people. For every aristocratic family living in splendour in one of Yorkshire's stately homes, surrounded by acres of parkland, there were hundreds of ordinary people who made their living working on these estates. Some people were employed as casual or seasonal labour, others lived in these great houses, working with loyalty for the same family year after year, even passing their profession down to their own children.

Unfortunately, most of us are not able to claim wealthy ancestors, with stately homes and vast estates. If we have any connection with a great estate, it will probably be that our ancestors were tenant farmers on the land, or perhaps one of an army of servants at the main house. This does not mean, though, that there will be nothing relating to our relatives in any archive belonging to a stately home. In fact, estate records can be some of the most rewarding to explore, because, as we shall see, they can reveal a great deal about our ancestors, even going as far as their personalities, reliability and describing the places where they lived.

WHERE TO FIND ESTATE RECORDS

Some of the documentation relating to Yorkshire's great estates is in private hands. But this does not mean that the information is not accessible. Many of the region's stately homes have archives and welcome researchers who contact them in advance. Some are so keen to foster good relations with the public that they put on exhibitions about what life was like living and working on the estate in years gone by. Visiting the estate where an ancestor lived or worked adds a new dimension to your research, allowing you to view their actual environment and imagine what their life would have been like there.

Many of the archives for Harewood House near Leeds are held at the Leeds branch of the West Yorkshire Archive Service. However, the Harewood House Trust on the Harewood estate also holds archives relating to the Lascelles family, who built and expanded the house. They were important sugar producers, holding substantial estates in the West Indies. Harewood House employed dozens of local people, either in the house itself or on the large estate. The papers held by the trust include election paraphernalia for Henry Lascelles's election campaign in 1807 and family papers, photographs and postcards for the nineteenth and twentieth centuries.

Further north, Kiplin Hall is a seventeenth-century stately home close to Richmond, North Yorkshire, which also holds archives relating to the hall and its grounds. The items kept in the archives include visitor books dating from the nineteenth and twentieth centuries, a family tree and letters and newspaper

Few of us can claim our ancestors lived in a mansion or castle (Pontefract Castle).

cuttings about the hall. There are also several inventories of the contents of Kiplin Hall at various points in its history. These would be particularly interesting to anyone who had an ancestor who worked in the house, showing what would have been in the rooms they might have cleaned and maintained. Some of Kiplin Hall's archives are also kept offsite, this time at the North Yorkshire County Record Office, Northallerton.

Many of the stately homes that keep archives have catalogued their holdings on the Access to Archives website (www.a2a.org.uk). But it can also be worth telephoning a stately home you are interested in to find out if they hold any archives, and if those archives are open to members of the public. If you are researching someone who worked there, they may well allow you to view the papers they hold.

However, many of the county's estate records have been placed in the hands of Yorkshire's local and county record offices. This particularly tends to be the case where an estate has fallen out of private ownership, perhaps when a family line ended or the occupants of the land could no longer afford the upkeep of a huge estate. As is usually the case when considering using records other than the traditional birth, marriage, death and census returns, the best starting point is the record office nearest the place you are researching. They should be able to advise whether they hold any relevant records and, if not, where they may be located.

Yorkshire is home to many spectacular monastic ruins such as Whitby Abbey.

MONASTERIES

Yorkshire is home to several large monasteries which owned vast holdings of land throughout the county. These estates also employed many of our ancestors, some of whom would have rented land from the monasteries, others who would have been employed as casual labour. By far the biggest monastic landowner in Yorkshire was Fountains Abbey. The abbey, near Ripon, North Yorkshire, was founded on a piece of desolate scrubland in 1132.

Through grants of land, for instance, from wealthy patrons such as King Henry II, the Cistercian order, to whom the monks of Fountains belonged, were able to extend their holdings. Fountains Abbey became famous for its sheep farming and, at the height of its prosperity during medieval times, owned around one million acres of land, stretching from Ripon through to the Lake District.

Gifts both large and small to monasteries were often recorded in charters, naming the benefactors and the gift they were donating. Many of these early documents have been published in collections, and can be found at local studies libraries and record offices.

Many early monastic documents mention individuals by name (Bolton Abbey).

TYPES OF ESTATE RECORDS

Fountains Abbey once owned a million acres of land.

Some of the most important records relating to land ownership will be kept at a local record office. These can include estate records such as rentals (which list tenants' names), and surveys, which again give a tenant's name and the acreage of the land they held. The Leeds branch of the West Yorkshire Archive Service, for example, holds the records for Fountains Abbey, Ripley Castle, Nostell Priory, Temple Newsham and Harewood House.

FAMILY LETTERS

Family letters can be an extremely revealing means of finding out more about our ancestors and the way they lived. Most letters that survive in Yorkshire, and indeed in any UK archives, were written by rich people. Before the nineteenth century, it was only wealthier people who had the means and education to correspond by letter. Where letters survive as part of a collection relating to a country estate or stately home, they can be of immense value if your ancestor was employed by the family concerned. Letters often related to business problems, to concerns or queries about staff and other family members, or to the running of an estate. As such, it is not unusual to find reference to named individuals as part of a collection of correspondence.

Title deeds are a big part of estate research and show the relationships between family members, the history of a property and the continuity of ownership. A title deed was a legal document that was drawn up to transfer property rights from one person to another.

Marriage settlements are also valuable, showing how men often married heiresses to keep wealth in their own families and to bring in further money and possessions. It could take months for the settlements to be drawn up and they often give great detail about the possessions that were part of the settlement.

MANORIAL RECORDS

Manorial records, where they survive, can be the family history researcher's best chance of finding a working-class person listed in estate archive material. The medieval manor was part of an estate, an administrative unit that could be anything from a small parcel of land to huge tracts of countryside, which covered several parishes. It had control over succession to parcels of land and acted as a court of law for various offences. This means that there is a chance of an ancestor being named in manorial records, perhaps as a landowner, tenant, someone who appeared in court or who sat on a jury.

Manorial records can include the recording of the death of a tenant and the subsequent payment of death duties by the person inheriting the land and title, fines levied for various offences and manorial surveys, which often include a list of tenants.

This all sounds promising, but it is important to remember that most medieval records are in Latin and survival of records is patchy. Nevertheless, if you are prepared to face such difficulties, the rewards can be great. The local record office for the area in which your ancestors lived is the best starting point for finding the location of any records that may not have survived. Even if they do not hold the relevant records, they will usually be able to advise who does.

The University of Hull archives hold a large collection of medieval manorial records. The archive's website www.hull.ac.uk divides the records alphabetically by place name, listing the various records held for each area, with the relevant dates. For example, records held for Willoughby in the West Riding include 15 court rolls covering the period 1485–1935, files of verdicts for 1815–52 and files of extracts from court rolls for the years 1865–90. Records for Driffield (East Riding) include jury verdicts from 1733 to 1817, a list of jurymen between 1750 and 1759 and call rolls for 1730 to 1817.

MANORIAL DOCUMENTS REGISTER

Anyone researching ancestors in Yorkshire is fortunate that the county is one of the few that has had manorial records digitalized on the Manorial Documents Register (www.mdr.nationalarchives.gov.uk). This is the official register of manorial documents in England and Wales and identifies where these records are located. The documents covered by the register include court rolls, surveys, maps and customs. The Manorial Documents Register indicates the type of manorial documents that have survived and shows where these are located.

The website offers a search facility using the name of a manor, the name of an English parish or the areas North, East and West Riding. Each of these choices can be accessed using the 'advanced search' option on the Manorial Documents Register home page. For example, selecting the English parish of

Beverley brings up 18 records. Some of the records are at the National Archives, or other archives outside Yorkshire, but the majority are at Yorkshire archives including the East Riding of Yorkshire Archives Service, Hull University Archives and the Yorkshire Archaeological Society.

Similarly, typing in the name of a manor, in another example, 'Fountains', brings up records for the Fountains Abbey estate in Ripon, which are held at the West Yorkshire Archive Service, Leeds. There are 32 records returned by the search and several of these look promising for anyone researching an ancestor who lived or worked on this estate. These include court books, a seventeenth-century calendar of freeholders to be returned as jurors and appointments of stewards and bailiffs between 1817 and 1912.

The site also allows searches using a combination of manor name, type of document and year, to allow more accuracy where some details are already known. Simply doing a search on one of the three ridings alone will bring up a list of dozens of manors in the area, allowing further research if the exact manor is not known.

The database contains full details of the archive which holds the record, including contact names, website details, opening hours and other accessions held.

WEST RIDING REGISTRY OF DEEDS

The West Riding Register of Deeds began in 1704 and was the oldest registry in England. The records are held at the Wakefield headquarters of the West Yorkshire Archive Service and contain several million deeds dating from 1704 to 1970, when the registry closed.

Researchers in West Yorkshire are fortunate in that, unlike most of the rest of the country, millions of deeds relating to the area have survived. These can provide information about an individual or family, including the type of property they owned, their occupation, other assets they held and businesses that belonged to them. The summaries of deeds held at Wakefield cover farms, houses, inns, shops and factories.

A deed is the title of ownership for a property and was drawn up to accompany the transaction of a sale of property between two parties. However, until 1970, it was not a legal requirement for a deed to be registered. The fact that the registry holds millions of deeds demonstrates that a good majority of deeds were registered, but it is important to realize that not all transactions were recorded.

The deed summaries are called memorials, and contain the main details from the property deed. They are indexed by name and place and held in bound volumes. To use the registry, you need the name of the owner of the property. Property was only registered when it changed hands and so if a property remained with one family for a long period of time it is unlikely to feature in the records. Leases of less than 21 years were not registered and registration did not always take place immediately after a property changed hands, so check a few years either side of your year of interest.

As well as listing previous deeds, tenants and sometimes former tenants, many deeds also recite previous deeds, going back over several generations. They may also name parcels of land, fields and whether or not the land was enclosed and whether it was pasture or enclosed land. Witnesses are also sometimes listed, who, as at weddings and baptisms, may be friends or family of the person concerned.

One fact that can cause research problems is that the deeds at the registry are arranged in volumes which are indexed by name, rather than property. This means that if you wish to trace the history of a property you will have little chance without the name of at least one of its owners.

If you don't have the name for any owner of the property you are researching, there are several avenues to pursue and staff at the registry are always happy to advise on the best course of action. First, it is worth trying to look up the property in the electoral registers or censuses to find out who was living there. It is possible, though, that the people registered there were tenants rather than owners, and so will not feature in the deeds indexes.

A second option is to use the records of the 1910 Financial Act. The Act was a property survey of maps and valuation books through which it is sometimes possible to trace a property. Deeds are only for outright sales, rather than leases, but sometimes do mention those staying in a property as tenants.

If the name of a property owner is found through either of these possibilities, it is then possible to begin your search, working backwards through time from the most recent date. The first name you have will have bought the property from someone else. Finding the first deed with that name on will give you the name of the person selling the property. They, in turn will have bought the property from another owner and so you are able to trace backwards.

The deeds often give interesting description of the property involved in the transaction. If you are able to find several deeds for the same building, it will be possible to compare the documents and see how the property changed and evolved. The name of a property or its number on the street may also have changed over the years. If a deed mentions a field number as part of a property, you may be able to view this on an Ordnance Survey map.

After 1970, there was a break of four years in which no deeds were registered, while arrangements were made to put in place a new system of registering property sale transactions. There are no property deeds records at all for this period. In 1974, it became a legal requirement to register property deeds and the land registry took over this responsibility. It is a boon for future family history researchers that the land registry indexed its deeds by property from the beginning, which will make tracing any deeds involved in a particular property's history much simpler.

MAPS

Maps are an often underused resource for family history researchers. Most record offices and libraries hold maps for their particular region and these can be invaluable in tracking the history of a town, property or estate. As with so many other areas of family history research, maps have their limitations as a resource, but as long as we are aware of those limitations, they can make a fantastic addition to any research.

Most of the region's libraries and record offices have collections of maps which can be consulted by family history researchers. These collections vary greatly in date, the area they cover and the detail each plan contains. The earliest useful map of Yorkshire is the 1577 Saxton's map. Other maps for particular areas of Yorkshire pre-date this one, but it is the first that can be regarded as being particularly helpful or accurate.

Although maps are excellent for showing what features or buildings appeared on a landscape at the time the document was created, it is important to be aware that, just because something doesn't appear on a map, it does not mean it didn't exist at that time. Before the nineteenth century, maps were often produced for specific reasons, and what appeared on a map could reflect this.

For example, a 1560 map of Leeds was produced to use in a court case involving the manor of Leeds. Several sites are missing from the map that are known to have existed at that time. This is because those sites were part of the town of Leeds, not the manor and, as such, were not considered relevant to the court case.

Because mapmaking required specialist skills, maps could be expensive to produce and so many mapmakers tended to copy earlier maps, which is another point to be aware of when using maps in family history research. For example, the 1577 Saxton's map of Yorkshire misses out estates such as Temple Newsham, on the outskirts of Leeds, that are known to have existed at the time the document was produced. This may be because the Temple Newsham estate did not appear on earlier drawings that were used to produce that map.

From the mid-eighteenth century onwards, mapping became a more independent industry and therefore the usefulness of maps increased and they could be relied upon to be more accurate and inclusive. Particularly useful is a John Warburton map of the 1720s, in which Warburton did his own surveying, which included climbing hills and church towers to assess angles and distances.

A Thomas Jefferies map dating from 1767 is the first accurate map of Yorkshire as we would know it. It shows features such as gentlemen's residences, which include the name of the relevant lord of the manor. Such a ploy helped the sale of maps to those featured on them. The Jefferies map is the best for Yorkshire before the advent of the Ordnance Survey maps that we still rely on today.

Maps for private estates are sometimes available, but as with so much in archives, whether they were produced at all, and if so whether they survived, is a matter of luck. Estate maps tend to run only until the 1850s, when Ordnance Survey maps reduced the need for new estate plans to be produced.

The Ordnance Survey mapping project began in 1800, amidst a climate of fear of an attack from France. The survey began in Kent, which was the area considered to be most under threat of an invasion, and reached Yorkshire by 1815. Ordnance Survey maps of the mid-nineteenth century are particularly valuable to researchers as they show detail way beyond anything we would expect nowadays. Some of the maps for the nineteenth century are on a 1:500 scale, around ten feet per mile, and these cover many Yorkshire towns and villages.

Tithe award maps were produced following the Tithe Commutation Act of 1836, whereby the church became entitled to cash rather than goods in payment for tithes. Maps were produced showing who owned what land and what each landowner was farming, to prove what tithes were owed to the church. These records could be used by anyone who wanted to buy a piece of land, so that they would be able to see what they would owe their future landlord.

BUSINESS AND COMMERCIAL ACTIVITY

Although we may imagine that those who owned large estates lived lives of ease as lords and ladies of the manor, the reality is that, particularly during the early years of an estate being established, many owners of stately homes and large estates had of necessity many commercial and business interests. It was often success in the commercial field which enabled people to buy these large houses and estates at all. As they grew in success and power, they might have hidden their commercial roots, but many estates, from medieval times onwards, were built on trade and industry.

Records for the Forbes-Adam family held at the University of Hull archives contain details of various types of commercial activity typical of a family that made its fortune before the Industrial Revolution. Among the family's estate archives is paperwork relating to Henry Thompson, a merchant who traded during the seventeenth century in York and overseas. Other estate papers held by the university contain information about attempts to mine coal in the Warter area of the East Riding.

Another important family, who were one of the wealthiest in Hull, were the Sykes, whose influence stretched throughout the Yorkshire Wolds area. The University of Hull archives also hold papers relating to this influential group of people. Their story shows how a family with relatively humble beginnings became one of the region's foremost mercantile dynasties.

The Sykes family began to amass their fortune in the West Riding, particularly through the Leeds wool trade. Daniel Sykes (1632–93) made his home in Hull and was mayor of the town twice, successfully working in finance and shipping. His son Richard (1678–1726) built upon his father's success to become one of Hull's wealthiest men. The papers in the archive relate mainly to the family's land and property interests in Hull and the Yorkshire Wolds. The collection includes an eighteenth-century letter book, which includes business accounts and details of goods shipped through Hull port. There are also hundreds of family letters covering subjects such as banking, finance and the administration of customer accounts.

CASE STUDY: ESTATE RECORDS AT NORTH YORKSHIRE COUNTY RECORD OFFICE

Estate records held by the North Yorkshire County record office provide a good indication of what a researcher could expect to find from the records of a large Yorkshire estate. As we shall see, there are documents which tell of how good a tenant was at paying their rent, about their family circumstances, the state of their property and even their personality. These types of details, which date to as early as the seventeenth century, would be something that most people researching their ancestors would never expect to find.

The records that follow demonstrate how generous landlords were towards their tenants and what happened to those who were unable to pay. They show what the job of rent collector entailed and how that person was treated by his employer when he was unable to collect rent from his tenants.

North Yorkshire's main industry has always been farming. North Yorkshire is quite different to the rest of the Yorkshire region in the pattern of its settlement. With the exception of the city of York, much of the habitation of this section of the county was made up of small towns and villages. One estate could cover several of these communities, with just one ruling family receiving rents from dozens of towns and villages.

This was obviously very different to crowded mill towns such as Leeds and Bradford or the engineering, mining and steel communities of South Yorkshire, where most people lived in crowded urban settings. Where court cases in these urban areas concentrated on things such as street brawls or disputes over refuse and pollution, cases for North Yorkshire tended to be more about boundary problems, theft of livestock and trespassing.

The North Yorkshire County Record Office holds an excellent collection of documents relating to the Swaledale estates of Lord Wharton from the sixteenth to seventeenth century. These archives also demonstrate what we can expect to find elsewhere in Yorkshire. The Wharton family were a wealthy group of people, with estates throughout the UK, including Cumberland, Yorkshire, Buckinghamshire and Ireland. Periodically, large landowners would commission a survey of their entire estates, some of which have survived, including Lord Wharton's survey of 1561. The surveys were intended to allow the landlord to see the value of his entire estate, but also, fortunately for family historians, provide information about those who lived on the land.

The surveys show how much each tenant was paying and most also give information about how much land was rented and what property was attached to that land. It is also possible to compare the rent each person or family was paying, to get an idea of how their estate compared to that of other tenants.

Rents on the Wharton estate seem to have varied somewhat, with two tenants in 1561 both paying 8 shillings. Thomas Abroe, a clerk, is listed as renting two houses and seven acres of land, whereas George Atkinson had one house and three acres of land for the same rent.

A lease document for Smarber Hall, one of Lord Wharton's properties, in September 1653, contains instructions of how the tenancy was to be run, giving an idea of some of the conditions landlords could impose. Tenants were told that if the rent was more than 14 days late, they could have goods 'distrained' and the landlord could repossess the premises after more than 40 days in arrears.

Tenants were to 'maintain houses, hedges and fences in good repair: landlord may enter to view and give orders and may repossess if repairs are not performed'. Not only did the tenants have to keep the inside of the hall in good order, they were also ordered to plant 26 trees each year, and fence them to keep cattle away. The list ends with a ruling that the red deer belonging to Lord Wharton were to be allowed to move around the premises 'without any annoyance, molestation or disturbance'. Presumably, the deer were also to be kept away from the fenced trees.

Viewing rules and regulations like these makes it easier to imagine what life must have been like on the estate, how strict the landlord was and what he expected of his tenants. Accounts of rents and receipts can be another excellent source of ancestor names, as well as giving information about the type of work that went on at an estate. Some of the items listed as being paid out to various tradespeople are very illuminating.

Accounts for the Wharton estate in 1699 include fees to a glazier and plumber, to a Richard Moorland for keeping the park wall in good repair, to Richard Wharton's wife for teaching six poor scholars at Kirby for half a year and to Mr Gunter and William Mortimer for a journey into Westmorland, Cumberland, Swaledale and back.

The Swaledale estate contained lead mines and the records at the North Yorkshire County Record Office include a record of Lord Wharton's instructions for keeping accounts at the mines and managing the lead works. This kind of original document not only throws light on how the works were run, but allows the family history researcher to discover more about how the miners were treated.

Wharton asked his agent to keep a list of all the men working at the mines and anyone who had an ancestor there would thank him, as he also requests that the clerk 'enter upon each of their names the worke they are most imployed in, and whence they come or where their famylies live if they have any'. If only all places of employment had kept such records.

Lord Wharton seems to have been extremely well versed in human nature, if his instructions for transporting money are anything to go by. He instructed that, when money was moved around the estate, no one was to go alone, but must have three or four companions. He even went as far as to suggest that landlords on the estate should provide a meal for the collectors, so that they would not be tempted to take anything from the money they were collecting, if they felt hungry.

Another letter to Lord Wharton from one of his collectors Philip Swale in 1683, reveals the difficulty that Swale had in collecting the rents, perhaps showing something of his own personality and the characters of those he was collecting from. He wrote:

> . . . though rents come slowly in, I canot helpe it: my sending and calling on the tenants is soe unpleaseing when they want money, that sometimes they avoyde to be spoken with.

A packhorse bridge enabled medieval traders to carry out business between different communities.

Another letter, this time from Wharton to Swale, from February 1684 or 1685, reveals Wharton's practical nature, as he seems to have realized that it was not always possible for Swale to collect the rents, due to the personal circumstances of tenants. He asked Swale whether there was any hope of Widow Broadrigs paying any part of her arrears, and urged Swale to be 'earnest with her' for the payment, if she was solvent.

He went on to ask about Robert Bell, who owed him hundreds of pounds. He told Swale he thought it best to take his stock and marketable goods and sell them off, to pay the debt. But 'because he has been an old tenant', Wharton urged Swale to leave him a cow or two for his family. Such details in what is a formal letter show the character of Lord Wharton, making it clear that he was realistic about whether people would pay, and ensuring even those who owed him considerable sums were left with something.

The correspondence between Swale and Wharton must be some of the best surviving seventeenth-century correspondence in Yorkshire, revealing as it does the personalities of the men and the people they did business with. In March 1684 or 1685, Swale described tenant Robert Carter as 'very honest and careful'. Marke Lambe, apparently had a 'hopefull young son' who was 'better humered than his father' and 'gaynes the love of neighbours, is married and lives handsomely'. Even those searching for nineteenth-century ancestors would be lucky to find personality quirks such as these written down on paper.

Swale obviously felt he could confide in his employer and the letter went on to talk about the difficulties of being a rent collector. He told Wharton it was difficult to find good tenants; even those who could pay took a while about it and would promise the money and gradually fall into arrears.

Maps can chart the history of well-known local buildings such as inns and hostelries (Black Bull Public House, Otley).

LOCAL NEWSPAPERS

Local newspapers are invaluable for many aspects of family history research, not least for following events 'as they happened'. It is always interesting to see how local, national and even international events were reported by a town or village's newspaper and most local studies libraries have a full range of news-papers on microfilm. Newspapers can give information about what was happening in a local community and the issues that would have been impor-tant to those living in it. Even advertisements can cast light on what people were buying, which local tradespeople served the town or village and where the main shops and services were located.

Newspapers were first used by traders who wanted to know the current market price for items such as grain and livestock. Even modest-sized towns often had more than one newspaper. Sometimes if there wasn't much national or international news, the newspapers would fill the pages with items about local trivia which can be a goldmine to family history researchers. Reports that may not make today's newspapers, but are invaluable for anyone searching for ancestors, could include someone winning a race at a fair, singing in a choir, acting in a village play, buying or selling property or passing an exam.

Local newspapers often covered a much wider area than you might think, encompassing several local towns and villages, in addition to the actual town where the paper was published. Items such as railway timetables and shop opening hours give an idea of day-to-day life. Smaller items can be amusing, such as one instance recorded in the *Yorkshire Observer* of 10 January 1924, which reports one woman's trip to a very amusing pantomime:

> Mrs Charles of South Street, Shipley, laughed so much at a pantomime at the Prince's Theatre that she dislocated her jaw. Dr Walker, who was in the theatre, advised her removal to St Luke's hospital where the jaw was attended to and Mrs Charles was able to go home.

Some of the articles which appear in local newspapers were often written in great seriousness, but can seem quite amusing to modern eyes, and give an insight into how people were treated. The *Yorkshire Post and Leeds Intelligencer* of 20 December 1880 carried a report about a drunken female. It may seem quite an absurd report to us, but it actually carries a serious message about how those under the influence of alcohol were treated:

> Jane Johnson, an old woman was brought before the Leeds Magistrates for the 143rd time . . . charged with being drunk. The old incorrigible was found by Police Constable Brew . . . sitting singing on the footpath on Call Lane. As the woman was too drunk to stand or walk the officer conveyed her to the police station in a wheelbarrow. The prisoner who said she was as sober as could be when the constable found her was sent to the workhouse.

Nowadays, we might expect someone with such a serious drink problem to receive help and support. Perhaps she would be released from the workhouse at a later date to commit her 144th offence. Little incidents like this provide relief from much more mundane reports of world trading and market prices which made up part of each issue of a newspaper.

Another way to use local newspapers is to examine their coverage of local accidents and incidents, such as that of Bradford's Zetland Mill disaster of 1924, in which four people died. The *Yorkshire Observer* gave much coverage to this event, including photographs, helping to build up a picture of what occurred on the days of the disaster and its aftermath and featuring those who were involved in the rescue operation.

The newspaper of 11 January, the day after the accident, devoted a whole page to reports about how three floors had crashed down into a basement at the mill. There are four large photographs, with captions, showing how quickly the photographers must have got to the scene. One caption reads:

> There were many pathetic scenes while the work of rescue was in progress. The picture shows one of the injured millgirls being carried to the ambulance.

Another photograph shows the twisted machinery that had buried some of the employees. Tom Mathers, reported the *Yorkshire Observer*, had the luckiest escape. He was in part of the building where the machinery crashed through several floors, and could have been crushed to death. Luckily, he was knocked between two bales of wool and protected by an iron girder. He managed to climb out after several hours, and astonished the rescuers by appearing suddenly at the bottom of their ladder and climbing to the top unaided.

There were many rescuers on hand after the collapse, including some Corporation workers who had been nearby clearing the snow from the roads and had rushed to the rescue with their shovels. However, many of the workers panicked and fled the scene, as the paper reports:

> The employees of the firm total 500 of both sexes and most of them who could not cooperate effectively in the rescue operation made for home as quickly as possible . . . this made a roll call impossible.

The tone in which the report is written is much more literary and flowery than we would expect today:

> From the depth of the mountain of wreckage rose the pitiful cries and groans of the imprisoned operatives, stimulating to Herculean efforts those whose mission it was to succour them.

The whole report brings to life a tragedy and shows how such a happening was reported to our ancestors who lived in the area. It is also worth checking the letters pages for the days and weeks after an incident or disaster. You will usually find discussion about the events, and people's reactions to them.

After the Poor Law Act of 1834, newspapers often carried details reports about the meetings of the boards of guardians and what was discussed there. Locally elected poor law guardians were placed in charge of the administration of workhouses in their area and of the treatment of the inmates. Reports of decisions taken at their meetings sometimes featured the names of inmates and workhouse staff, as well as giving information about the workhouse itself. There is more information about using other sources to trace ancestors who resided in a workhouse in Chapter 7.

Newspaper announcements about birth, engagements, marriage and deaths became more common from the beginning of the nineteenth century. However, it is important to remember that readers had to pay to insert such advertisements and so they were often beyond the means of poorer people.

Birth notices usually gave the mother's maiden name and information about where and when the christening would take place. Before the Second World War, marriage notices for wealthier people often gave information about the dowry that the bride was bringing to the marriage. Reports about the weddings of wealthy or influential people were classed as news in local papers and often went into great detail about the bride and groom, naming their guests, the best man, bridesmaids and ushers and even sometimes service-people such as the organist and choir.

Death notices can be particularly helpful, as they usually gave a brief obituary of the person concerned, sometimes citing any hobbies and interests they had and naming any clubs of which they had been a member. In wartime, local newspapers often carried names of service people who had been killed in action or gave details of those who had won medals for military service and bravery.

Another source of names in local newspapers are the pages devoted to the crimes that had taken place in the district. Reports of crimes were often followed with great fascination by the public and the amount of detail about murders and injuries can seem quite lurid and morbid to our modern eyes. Nevertheless, this detail means that even those who played a minor role, such as helping to bring about an arrest, will be mentioned by name in the report.

As we have seen, advertisements are often a great source for finding out about current prices for things that people were buying and selling and seeing what sorts of goods and services were on offer to our ancestors. The earliest newspapers sometimes placed adverts offering a reward for the return of stolen goods and even for the return of runaway servants or apprentices. If your ancestor was one such person, you would be pleased to find that the advert often contained information about the person's physical appearance and even their clothing.

TRADE DIRECTORIES

Trade directories, the forerunners of publications such as today's telephone directories, can be surprisingly full of information about what life was like in the town or village where your ancestors lived. The first commercial directory was compiled in London in 1677, and consisted simply of a list of London merchants. But soon printers began to produce books or pamphlets with the names and addresses of tradespeople living in a particular town.

They can give many clues to the commercial makeup of a particular area, not least through the listings of tradespeople that comprise the bulk of the book, and can show, for example, whether a particular area had a specialist trade or industry, and how many different types of merchants traded there.

The trade directories also often have summaries about the areas they covered in terms of population, the acreage of the area and even its political makeup. They can give a potted history of the town, listing schools and churches, together with names of their respective head teachers or pastors.

It is also possible to trace the history of a particular street by seeing how long it has been listed in consecutive directories, which can give a clue as to when the street began its life and also to trace what businesses were there and how long they lasted. If your ancestor lived or traded on one of those streets, it is even more interesting to trace the businesses that operated around them and discover who their neighbours were.

The earliest Yorkshire directories began with *Baines's Yorkshire*, dating back to 1822. The *Kelly's Directory of the West Riding* for 1889 gives a good idea of what you can expect to find in a nineteenth-century directory. Although these type of publications were written with the aim of grouping businesses into one book, and so selling the directory to the public, they have much to attract anyone researching their family tree.

The *Kelly's Directory* for 1889 is in several separate volumes and part 7 began by giving a description of the town of Sheffield, stating that 'the great seat of the cutlery, plated goods and other hardware and iron and steel manufacturers is a large and populous market town'. The directory mentioned how many members of parliament had been returned for each town, in Sheffield's case five, and went on to give a potted history of the town's transport system, stating that railways reached Sheffield in 1838, with the creation of the Sheffield and Rotherham railway.

The directories can often seem quite tightly packed with information, and are perhaps not set out in the user-friendly manner we might expect today. But it is well worth checking through the information sections located before the listings of homes and businesses, as this is where valuable data are situated.

One of the sections in the Sheffield volume concentrated on places of worship, listing each church, chapel or other place of worship in the town, with information on these religious buildings and their history. The entry for St Luke's Church on Dyer Hill tells us that it was founded in July 1846, and the church, built in 1878, cost £10,000 to build. The vicarage cost £2,000 and the pastor at that time was a Revd Frederick Williams. The church is described as being in the early pointed style, with 100 foot tower containing a single bell.

Even a short entry such as that for St Luke's thus gives a lot of information which it could be difficult to find elsewhere. Also, having a full list of churches on a few pages allows you to compare the place of worship your ancestor may have attended with other churches in the location.

The next section in the directory is 'municipal and administrative buildings and offices'. Among the buildings described is Sheffield's Police Station at Castle Green. The directory states that the station cost over £16,000 to construct and had 34 cells, which could house over 70 prisoners. The officers making up the Sheffield police force, according to the directory, were a chief constable, two superintendents, 14 inspectors, four detective inspectors, five detectives, 31 sergeants and 308 police constables.

The 'public institutions and monuments' section of the directory includes a list of Sheffield's dozens of theatres. The Theatre Royal on the corner of Tudor

St and Arundel St is described as having 2,000 seats, costing over £8,000 to rebuild in 1880 and was leased at the time by a Mr W H Daw.

Sheffield Borough Hospital for Infectious Diseases is one of the buildings described in the 'hospitals and nursing institutions' section of the guide. Again, the description given is very detailed, so anyone who had an ancestor who was a patient or who was employed at one of the town's hospitals would find plenty of information, including clues as to what types of illnesses were prevalent in the district at the time. The hospital charged 10 shillings per week for adults, and 5 shillings for children under 14. It admitted 748 patients during 1887 and 646 of those were suffering from smallpox.

Another place of good work described is the Sheffield Girls' Friendly Society Lodge, on Havelock St. The society boasted Queen Victoria as its patron and offered

> . . . a home where members of the society and other young women of respectable character may obtain a comfortable lodging either for one night or for a longer period.

The society offered sewing and knitting classes where girls could take clean garments to mend, as well as a lending library and singing classes.

As you can see, going through even a few pages of a directory, it is possible to build up a picture of what life was like in that town. The next section of the directory gives information about population, in this case for Sheffield. The guide stated that Sheffield had a total of 91,806 inhabitants in 1881, compared to 91,361 in 1871. Alongside the population tables are geographical and demographic descriptions of the various towns and villages that made up the Sheffield area. The directory also gave a list of certain private residents who chose to be listed, together with their addresses. Some have their first name listed alongside their surname, others just their title and an initial.

The directory went into detail about arrangements for the collection and delivery of mail and modern-day readers will probably be surprised at how comprehensive the postal system was. The directory listed where post boxes were located in the town and how often they were emptied (usually twice a day). There were also at least two deliveries a day of letters to the local post office.

Most directories contain information about the schools in each town or village, which can stimulate further research, perhaps at a local record office, once you have found out which schools existed in your ancestor's local area.

One way to bring research to life is to look at the listings in a directory which was compiled at the time your ancestor was living in a town and look up the different trades and professions listed on a street near where they lived. For example, Northgate in Halifax, West Yorkshire, was listed in *Kelly's Directory* as a street full of tradespeople of every description, a variety of shops and businesses that we would be hard pressed to find today. The vendors included a grocer, chemist, watch maker, beer retailer, pork butcher, London and North Western goods receiving house, oil and lamp dealer, stationer, tea dealer, wool stapler, outfitter, boot maker, wool and waste dealer, wardrobe dealer, hairdresser, book seller, basket maker and brass founder.

Such a search can also throw up interesting patterns about the makeup of the area. Halifax was well known as a centre for textile production and sales, which is reflected in the type of businesses on Northgate at that time.

The first volume of the *Kelly's Directory* for 1889 had general information about the whole area covered by the directories and listed the principal estates in the West Riding, giving the name of the house or hall and its owner. There was an index to commercial prospectuses, many of whom also placed adverts in the directory. This was one of the ways the directory made its money. There was also a section on how parliamentary representation in the area was organized, with parts of the chapter showing how many MPs were returned by each town or borough.

The army was also represented, with information about the different regiments in the various towns and their commander. Fairs and markets were listed, with information about how often these events were held. The listing for

A market cross was often the centre of a community (Thirsk market place).

Holmfirth in West Yorkshire shows that the town had agricultural markets in March, May and October.

Part of the directory was given over to statistics about the region the guide covered, which can help to show what sort of a society your ancestor lived in, how agricultural or urban it was and how densely populated. The 1889 guide went into a great deal of information about the farming situation, stating that over 208,000 acres of land in the West Riding were given over to corn and cereal production, with 2,652 acres to market gardens and over 803,000 acres of permanent pasture. There were over 122,000 cows and 71,000 pigs, with over 59,000 owners holding lands amounting to less than an acre and 17,000 owning more than an acre.

Because the population of parts of Yorkshire often changed so fast, it is worth comparing the information about populations and agriculture over a few different editions of a directory, to see just how quickly the data altered. When a population rose rapidly over a short space of time there were often social problems, as we shall see in the next section.

UNREST

Many towns and cities have experienced periods of disturbance and unrest, often related to the large numbers of people living in overcrowded conditions. Where an episode of unrest occurred in a town, it would have been reported, sometimes at length, in the local newspapers and sometimes made the national newspapers as well.

A good example is given by media reports of the Rotherham election riots of 24 July 1865, when the police had to call in military reinforcements to quell an angry crowd. *The Times* newspaper carried an extensive report, which as well as naming many of those involved on both sides of the riot provided details of how such incidents were dealt with and the consequences for those who instigated them.

The Times article reported that the riot had begun when a crowd of people took exception to the blue Tory colours and were angered by a man named Walker who decided to make his way through a group of people dressed in blue. The crowd turned against him and when the police intervened, using truncheons, the riot began.

The crowd, which had assembled in the High St and Westgate, began to throw stones, damaging several properties, including the Crown Inn and a hairdressing and hatter premises belonging to a Mr Evans. The police superintendent Mr Gillett was cut on his head during the stone throwing and it was decided that the police should retreat to the Crown Inn and call for reinforcements.

The 15th Hussars arrived from Sheffield barracks and entered the crowd, using the flats of their swords to try to disperse the mob. *The Times* reported:

The men who were in High Street were constantly called upon to repel the rushes of the mob, who manifested great excitement, and we saw several stones thrown at the soldiers as they stood at the top of Westgate.

The reading of the Riot Act by Justice of the Peace G Chambers did nothing to quell the excitement and the newspaper reported that officers began to clear the streets using the points of their swords. A Thomas David of Parkgate was badly injured and denied the accusations of the police that he had been one of the instigators of the riot.

LOCAL COUNCIL RECORDS

All local councils kept records of their proceedings, and many are available for consultation at record offices or local history libraries throughout the region. Far from being the dry, repetitive documents that we might imagine, they can contain fascinating information about the areas and populations the councils covered, much of which is not available anywhere else.

The annual reports of committees of Leeds City Council are kept at the Leeds Local Studies Library. Each volume comprises hundreds of pages, some of which contain graphs and data which are of little use to the family historian. However, it is well worth persevering with a study of these documents, as much of what the committees report can be of great interest.

The first section of a 1936/7 volume is devoted to public spending and money coming into the council. Leeds City Council collected over £350,000 in rents in the financial year 1936/7, with £14,886 arrears uncollected. The listings of government grants made to the council is a good indicator of what causes were receiving attention; Leeds Council was given £2,893 for pedestrian crossings, £302 for an improvement scheme of West St, an 'unhealthy area', and £69 for air raid precautions, which included an anti-gas van. Clearly a build-up to war was being anticipated even two years before the outbreak of the Second World War.

Although you are unlikely to find an ancestor named in council documents, they are an excellent way of gaining background information about how the authorities looked after those in their care and what the priorities of those authorities were. Social welfare, poverty relief, housing schemes and leisure time are all covered by council reports.

The next part of the Leeds City Council report for the financial year 1936/7 gives details about unemployment in the city and the relief schemes provided. A table of unemployment makes interesting reading, showing that 1921, nationally a year of great poverty, saw over 36,000 out of work in the city, dropping drastically to just over 10,500 unemployed five years later.

The annual report of the public assistance committee is included in the volume for 1936/7, and gives an excellent indication of what officials did to try to alleviate poverty and distress. The document reports the difficulties experienced by many people who were collecting their public relief money: 'The distance of the estates from the existing relief stations necessitates expenditure in travelling which can be ill afforded by relief recipients.' The fact that this difficulty had been noted shows that the committee was prepared to show at least some compassion to those claiming money. It was decided, noted the annual report, to make sure that relief stations were situated nearer to where those claiming relief lived.

The next part of the report went on to give details about the city's poor houses and children's homes. The councillors had noted that the poor houses were now seeing fewer able-bodied men and women than previously and that most inhabitants were either aged or incapable of work because of sickness. There were 298 children in Leeds children's homes for the period 1936/7 and it was reported that the children had been taken to a holiday camp at Abergele, where they had a 'happy and enjoyable holiday'. The report even lists in which trade each child was employed once they had been discharged from the home. Most of the girls went into domestic service, with the majority of the boys being apprenticed into a trade, most commonly farming and tailoring.

The health and housing committee reports were included with the Leeds City Council reports for the same year. The health committee noted that 31.24 inches of rain had fallen in the city that year, compared to 31.70 inches the previous year. There had also been 1,142 hours of sunshine – compared to the 1,368 hours Leeds enjoyed the year before.

Small details such as these can tell us so much about the community and environment in which our ancestors lived. The same report gave information about the number of births (7,340) and deaths (6,666), in 1936, again allowing the researcher to make comparisons with other years when the deaths may have been higher than births, for example, a few years after 1936, during the Second World War.

The findings of the housing committee are very revealing, underlining the fact that the 1930s were a time of slum clearance in some of Britain's biggest cities. The report begins by listing which streets were under enquiry for a slum clearance. These included Salem Place and Central Kirkstall Rd, both of which were listed as 'unhealthy areas'.

According to the report, the previous year had seen 1,672 houses and businesses demolished under the Housing Act of 1936. Several Acts of Parliament during the 1930s had passed the responsibility for the provision of housing for working-class people from the government to councils. For the first time, local authorities, working with building societies, were to provide housing to rent out, on a large scale. The Housing Acts did stipulate that the government would continue to subsidize slum clearance. Clearly, the problem of substandard housing had not been completely solved in Leeds by 1937, as the document states that 835 dwellings in the city had been fumigated by HCN gas at a cost of £31 per dwelling.

York city archives also hold substantial records relating to the York City Council and its predecessor authorities from the twelfth century onwards. The records are divided into various departments including education, engineers, health, housing and museums. As you would expect from a city with such a well-charted history, there are centuries' worth of council committee minutes and various charters and records about the city's poor.

York's rural district vaccination registers cover the period 1872 to 1907 and include the names and occupations of all who were vaccinated during this time. It is interesting to note the occupations changing from rural-based work, when the registers commence, to more industrial-based jobs at the end of the nineteenth century.

One of those vaccinated was a John Daniel, for whom letters and a vaccination certificate survive. According to the records, he was 'residing in a van' and his father Isaac Foster was a travelling showman and acrobat. Another letter for 1905 has a Mr Wrigglesworth writing to Mr Horsfield about a child who was considered too delicate to vaccinate.

LOCAL STUDIES LIBRARIES

As we have seen, local authority records and local newspapers help to build up a picture of life for our ancestors. The region's local studies and local history libraries are another excellent way to fill out the bare facts obtained from traditional family history sources such as censuses and birth, marriage and death certificates.

Most local studies and local history libraries are concerned with the study and history of a local area right up to the present day. They will contain both primary sources (such as census returns or newspaper reports) and secondary data (such as books about the area or biographies of local personalities). It is often possible to use the facilities without being a member of the library and an appointment is not usually needed. Many of the libraries have card index systems, so a subject such as 'workhouses' or 'schools' can be looked up to reveal what items the library holds on that particular field of interest.

It would be impractical to list all of the holdings at the region's dozens of local studies and local history libraries. The following description of the holdings of Sheffield Local Studies Library gives a good indication of what type of material you can expect find at a Yorkshire local or family history library. The library at Sheffield is based in the city centre and is concerned with both present-day and historic Sheffield. It contains over 30,000 volumes about life in the city and Sheffield people past and present. There are collections of local newspapers dating back to 1787, biographies of Sheffield people, street and trade directories and electoral registers from 1841 onwards. The library also holds a collection of recordings of oral memories and there are facilities for users to listen to the cassette tapes in the library.

Sheffield Local Studies Library.

The library holds both primary and secondary source materials that would be useful in family history research. Among the most useful and unusual primary source materials are the collections of local pamphlets, which are bound into volumes. These vary widely in subject from memorials of Sheffield people to the running of some of the city's clubs and societies.

The pamphlets are all A5 size or smaller and many are illustrated with photographs and detailed sketches. One of the pamphlets was produced by the wife of Perry Rawson, who was a justice of the peace in Sheffield. Rawson died in 1909 and the booklet commemorated his life, including biographical details, testimonies from friends and colleagues and details of Rawson's working years. It was illustrated with a photograph and delicate Edwardian drawings.

Another pamphlet concerns the rules of the Richmond Lodge of Odd Fellows and was published in 1863. The lodge was a group which allowed working men to pay a weekly insurance in case of sickness or death, roughly equivalent to modern-day life insurance policies. The lodge is described as being for the working men of Handsworth and having had over 80 members. The group met weekly and elected officers were fined 6d if they were late for a meeting or 1s if they didn't attend at all. Anyone wishing to pay into the lodge had to be over 18 and under 40 years of age. Certain trades were excluded from the insurance – needle or fork grinding, lead work 'or any other trade detrimental to health'. The book of rules stated that sickness benefit would not be paid out to a member in the case of fighting, dog fighting or wrestling, drunkenness, race running, poaching or venereal disease. There was also a curfew for anyone in receipt of the sickness benefits, which was 7 p.m. between September and March and 9 p.m. in the lighter months of March to September.

Also collected at the library are the bound volumes of city by-laws dating from the mid-nineteenth century onwards. Reading through these rules gives a vivid impression of what life was like in Sheffield at the time they were written, and what issues were important to the people in charge of the particular facility concerned.

A booklet produced in 1869 for the public baths tells of a time when few people had a bathroom at home. Baths for the 'labouring classes' were priced at 1d for a cold bath and 2d with warm water. Children were allowed into a bath up to four at a time, at a charge of 2d cold and 4d warm. 'Baths of a higher class' were charged at 3d for a cold slipper bath and 6d with warm water. The baths, stated the by-laws, 'shall be open to all persons except such as are intoxicated, disorderly or diseased'. A list of fines shows what could go wrong, even in a bath house; bringing in liquor carried a penalty of 10s, there was a 40s fine for profane swearing, violent, disorderly, indecent or insulting behaviour and a 5s fine for using soap in the public swimming bath.

Another set of by-laws dated 1878 concerned porters and drovers. The rules show that, by the 1880s, the carriage and transport industries were already highly regulated in the city. All porters were required to have a licence and had to paint that licence number on their cart. They also had to wear a badge of office on their left arm. There is a list of charges for various fares, ranging from 6d to carry an errand or message no more than 1,000 yards, to 1s 6d for carrying a parcel or luggage no more than 2,500 yards. The charges for drovers shows that Sheffield still had a rural aspect, even during this time of industrialization; a drover could charge 5s for driving 200 animals up to a mile from the railway station to a field; clearly, there were fields within a mile of the city centre where the station was located. The highest charge was for driving 800 animals up to a mile, which cost £1 and must have been a spectacular site in a busy town centre.

Secondary sources at the library include school, hospital and business histories for Sheffield and surrounding areas. Many of the business histories relate to the steel and engineering industries for which Sheffield was so renowned. They are an excellent way to find out how the industries began and developed in the town, and how they came to employ so many thousands of people.

Chapter 5

FROM SPORT TO SHOPPING: LEISURE TIME

Life may sometimes have been a struggle for our ancestors, but there were plenty of chances to have fun as well. In the days before television and radio, sports, amateur dramatics and cinema offered ordinary people the chance to escape the reality of daily life.

Morrisons Supermarket was the first experience of supermarket shopping for many Yorkshire people (© Morrisons Supermarkets PLC).

From amateur plays in village halls, to extravagant pantomimes in theatres such as Bradford's Alhambra, there was often a wide range of entertainment to choose from. Information about local sports clubs, the productions of amateur dramatics societies and the activities of countless clubs and societies was regularly reported in local newspapers, often with photographs and names of the participants. Some of the archives of these clubs and societies have been deposited for public research, as we shall see in this chapter.

THEATRE

Yorkshire people have always enjoyed a good show and the region is the birthplace of celebrated performers including actor Charles Laughton and music hall star Gertie Millar. Large theatres such as the York Theatre Royal regularly hosted plays and pantomimes featuring big names of the day, but also staged smaller scale shows that included amateur performers, particularly from local dramatic societies. Such events were eagerly supported and often appeared in the town's local newspaper.

Most of the region's local record offices contain programmes, playbills and posters from Yorkshire theatres. These usually featured a full cast list, often with photographs, and also included orchestra members and even biographies of some of the performers.

The Leeds Local Studies Library holds one of Yorkshire's biggest collections of programmes and playbills, dating back to the eighteenth century. It also includes items from circuses that visited the region. Many of the bills list the performers involved and most give vivid descriptions of what the shows included, giving a real flavour of what entertainments our ancestors would have looked forward to.

A playbill for March 1850 describes a circus performance being held 'for the benefit of the clown, Jackson'. Jackson seems to have been retiring from the profession and wanted to make sure his parting would be remembered, although the treatment of the unfortunate prize animal would be frowned upon today:

> Jackson intends this being a night of fun – to be given away, the prize of a fat pig! The first six that draw the prize to enter the ring and then be blindfolded, have a small stick in their hands and the first that hits the pig to claim him.

Tickets ranged from 3d in the upper gallery, to 2s in the boxes and it was announced that 'Jackson' would be giving his final performance at the show.

The website www.leodis.net, a Leeds Library and Information Service project, has a searchable database of old playbills, and it is possible to buy copies of the posters, most of which feature the names of actors and actresses.

Theatre performances were naturally subject to disruption during wartime, particularly during the bombing raids that Yorkshire towns suffered during the Second World War. But an article in the *Yorkshire Post* of January 1941 illustrates how performers usually adhered to the old showbiz adage that 'the show must go on'. The paper carried an interview with performer Francis Laidler, a well-known face in the theatres of Yorkshire. Laidler stated that he would not allow hostilities to affect any performances he was part of and would continue to perform in Leeds, London, Bradford and Sheffield, 'yet feeling deeply for those members of his companies who have suffered from German air attacks'. The report goes on to say that theatre rehearsals were often disrupted by air raids, but when a raid interrupted rehearsals for *Mother Goose* in Sheffield, all members of the cast voted to continue, and ignored the sirens.

Sheffield archives also hold a number of nineteenth- and twentieth-century playbills. Some of these are almost 2 feet tall, and would have been displayed outside the theatres and in other public places. As well as listing the players in the performances, the posters included adverts from local businesses who would have paid to be included on the playbill. The services offered by these businesses range from breweries to shoemakers. The adverts are interesting not only for the names of prominent local firms, but for the special offers and prices that were often included in the advertisements.

One of the posters is for a performance of *French Maid*, which was held at Sheffield's Theatre Royal in October 1897. Ticket prices ranged from a private box at £2 2s to a seat in the gallery for 4d. The poster also gave details of the late trains running back to towns such as Chesterfield, Rotherham and Doncaster after the performance.

SPORTS CLUBS

The activities of local sports clubs can often be traced through the pages of local and regional newspapers. The proceedings of sports club meetings were sometimes reported through local papers, as an article in the *Yorkshire Observer* from January 1924 shows. Ilkley may have had a reputation as a genteel spa town, but there had been some complaints about certain of the town's rugby supporters that were brought up at a meeting of the Yorkshire Rugby Union Club held at Leeds's Metropole hotel:

> Arising out of a case of a reported Ilkley player it was decided that a letter should be sent to the Ilkley committee asking it to try and make its supporters conduct themselves in a more sportsmanlike manner.

Many sports clubs were affiliated to places of work, with football, rugby and cricket being particularly popular team sports. Employers often encouraged out-of-hours sports activities, believing that they would foster good relations between employees and keep workers out of trouble. The records of such clubs have usually been deposited wherever the rest of the company archives are. The games and matches played by the clubs were often featured in the company magazine, with employees who did not actually take part giving up their free time to cheer along colleagues in their games.

COUNCIL REPORTS

As we saw in Chapter 4, town or city council annual reports can be a good source of information about community life and the environment our ancestors experienced. The reports often contain information about the leisure area of council work, which included parks and swimming pools, art galleries and libraries and civic events.

The annual report of the Libraries and Arts Committee for Leeds City Council in 1936/7 set out a programme of events that had been organized by the committee at various points around Leeds. These included a Yorkshire Artists' Annual Exhibition, which was opened by Major Milner, and public lectures at Kirkstall Abbey House Museum. The subjects covered at the Kirkstall Abbey lectures are diverse and it is interesting to see what drew in the crowds of 1930s Leeds; the lectures were on 'Flight', 'English country and town life in the 14th century', 'The old Leeds stage – its plays and players' and 'Leeds boys in other lands'.

The report went on to give information about the popularity of the city's lending libraries. We are used to hearing about the decline of our library services and the dangers of technology overtaking traditional pastimes such as reading, but according to the report for Leeds in 1936, the library was one of the city's most popular amenities. Over a year, the Leeds libraries issued 3,350,823 books, an average of 11,132 books for each day the libraries were open. The bulk of this lending was adult fiction. Apparently, there had been a problem with new books being in great demand, which led the author of the report to advise that it 'would be of advantage to both library and readers if it were more generally realised that much that is old is better than much that is new'. Such personal comments in an otherwise impersonal document help bring to life something which was of obvious concern to library staff.

The next report in the Leeds council papers for 1936/7 is by the Parks, Allotments and Cemeteries Committee. From the outdoor pastimes that were provided by the council, the city had taken £1,880 in tennis receipts and £1,443 in bowling green admissions for the previous financial year. At Roundhay Park, £78 was collected from donkey rides and £1,375 from boating fees. The report also contains information about an annual swimming gala held at the city's Roundhay Park. Swimming was obviously a popular pastime for Yorkshire children and Leeds had 80 summer and 52 winter swimming clubs.

Leeds children swept the board at the swimming gala of 1936, with 40 points to Bradford's and Sheffield's 22 points each.

Council papers are a very valuable source of background information about life in a city or town. Although they do not usually contain individual names, they give lots of facts and figures which can help place your research into context and bring a particular period to life. Everyday life is often covered in great detail, making council documents an unparalleled, and often underused, background research source.

THE YORKSHIRE CO-OPERATIVE SOCIETY

Thousands of our ancestors would have shopped at Co-operative stores, which were located in towns and villages throughout Yorkshire. The Co-operative movement was founded in Rochdale in 1844 and Yorkshire Co-operative Society branches were some of the most enthusiastic in the country. Still in existence today, the society was very much a part of everyday life for thousands of Yorkshire people through the services it offered to both rural and urban communities.

Many Co-operative societies have donated their records to the local record offices of their nearest town and we will examine some of these later in this section. Because membership was open to anyone, of whatever financial means, many of our ancestors would have used the facilities offered by the societies. The Co-operative offered funeral services, education and social activities for the young and old. Some of the archive material of interest to anyone searching for information about an ancestor includes the pamphlets which were regularly published by Co-operative societies, detailing histories of the various groups, which often name staff and committee members.

Co-operative societies offered help to groups of people in times of need, such as in the aftermath of a local industrial disaster, and information about fundraising efforts and the people who helped and who were helped is often kept with the records of the Co-operative society concerned.

We are familiar with the Co-op shops that still stand on our high streets, but for our nineteenth-century ancestors, shopping as part of a co-operative rather than being reliant on a single tradesperson was a new idea. Co-operative shops quickly caught on and became popular in towns that had industrialized quickly and had large populations crammed into small areas. Before the Co-ops were established, people had been victim to unscrupulous local merchants who tricked shoppers by adulterating food with items such as chalk to make it seem heavier and by charging extortionate prices because there was nowhere else for people to shop.

Co-op stores stated that all shoppers were members of their local Co-operative society and had a vote at meetings. All members received a dividend (popularly known as the divi), in proportion to how much they had spent at the shop. There was a 'no credit' policy, with the shops promising to supply good quality provisions and services.

Although the Co-op shops became a valuable local resource, those who sourced food for the stores during the nineteenth century struggled to obtain goods at fair prices as other private merchants jealously tried to force them out of business. It was for this reason that the Co-operative Wholesale Society was founded. The wholesale society manufactured goods specifically for Co-operative stores and so successful was this manufacture and trade formula that by the end of the nineteenth century there were over 1,000 Co-operative societies in the UK. The Co-operative movement was particularly popular in northern industrial towns, with some 300 stores trading in Yorkshire and Lancashire during the late nineteenth century. The Co-operative Wholesale Society's huge buying power enabled each individual store to stock goods at a reasonable price.

The records of the Gargrave Co-operative Society, North Yorkshire, are held at Bradford archives and are a typical example of the type of records that were created by society members. The Gargrave group, in common with most of the other Co-operative societies, held weekly meetings at which anything of concern or interest could be discussed. One hardback book in the collection for Gargrave covers the period 1943–8 and mentions members by name. An entry for February 1944 stated that present at the meeting were Messrs Grey, Mitchell, Bateson, Kirkbright, Bradley, Saunders and Sinclair. Mr Bradley paid £2 that evening to become a member and was accepted as a club member. He was also listed later in the year as having being employed to deliver coal to some of the members at the rate of 11d per hour.

The Co-operative society encouraged all its members to be active in local charities and those which were supported by the Gargrave branch are mentioned throughout the meeting book. On different occasions donations were given to the police orphanage, Leeds General Infirmary and Barnados homes. Seeing which charities were supported by this branch of the society shows where member's interests and sympathies lay.

Much of what it reported in the meetings stayed the same from month to month. But there were always special incidents recorded and which are a fascinating insight into village life in the 1940s. One member's complaint in November 1946 concerned the fact that customers in the drapery department of the Co-op store were loitering in the department after they had finished shopping.

As the minutes book runs for several consecutive years, it is possible to follow the progress of members. Mr Kirkbright is one of the first to be mentioned in 1943 and an entry for September 1947 notes that 'at the outset of the meeting all stood in silence for a short time as a token of sympathy for the late Mr Kirkbright'. This type of entry could be invaluable to anyone who was unsure of an ancestor's date of death, giving an accurate month and year with which to begin the search for a death certificate.

One incident which took up almost the whole of a January 1946 meeting was the case of Messrs Driver and Ware. These two men were recorded in the minutes as having refused to serve tobacco. The entry for that date stated 'they will be given until Thursday to alter their attitude, if they persist in their present attitude they will be told to attend next Thursday's meeting. If not cooperating by then will be given a week's notice.' The incident is not referred to in subsequent entries and so presumably the two unfortunate men gave into the pressure and sold tobacco once again.

NATIONAL FAIRGROUND ARCHIVE

In an age before cinema and TV, travelling fairs were a popular and much anticipated form of entertainment. Particularly popular with audiences were the freak shows and menageries of unusual animals from Commonwealth countries. Animals on show to the public included hyenas, panthers and leopards, as well as collections of reptiles, particularly snakes. Most towns would have had at least one fair or circus pay a visit during the summer months, usually at holiday times, when the area's mills and factories had closed for a few weeks.

If your ancestors worked as part of a permanent or travelling fair, you may find that they can be difficult to track through censuses and other official records, because of the transitory nature of their lifestyle. Moving from place to place frequently meant that many fair folk either deliberately or inadvertently escaped official records on many occasions. Even if records such as birth, marriage, death certificates and census records exist, it can be difficult to pinpoint where to expect to find a travelling ancestor in order to know where to start your search. The National Fairground Archive is a rich source of information about circus and fair workers and can be of great help in researching this way of life. The archive was set up in 1994 and is housed at the library of the University of Sheffield.

The idea to form a national archive of documents and memorabilia relating to fairgrounds and circuses came from Vanessa Toulmin, who is now the archive's research director. Dr Toulmin spent her childhood in a fairground family and is only too aware of how easily memories, documents and photographs can be lost or forgotten, particularly in a travelling community which does not have a permanent home. Toulmin used her connections within the fairground to gather much of the material available to researchers, including a number of valuable and rare items. The oldest document dates from the thirteenth century, and concerns the granting of a charter for a fair. Fairs were particularly popular in the nineteenth century and the archives are particularly strong for this period.

The National Fairground Archive is so well respected that material has been donated by the Fairground Association of Great Britain, the Fairground

Society, the Circus Friends Association and the Showmen's Guild of Great Britain, as well as being home to the private collections of circus and fairground families. Paper-based materials at the archive include a complete run of the *World's Fair* newspaper, which was first published in 1904. The paper is effective in tracking changes in fairground life through its pages of reports on different fairs, death and marriage announcements and names of showmen attending various fairs.

Also included in the paper are advertisements for labour and for buying and selling caravans and stalls, giving a good indication of how prices changed over the years. Job adverts also feature. So if you find a fairground ancestor listed on a particular census doing a certain fairground-related job, you might be able to find that job in the recruitment section of one of those publications, with a description of the type of work it involved.

Another valuable research tool is the *Fairground Mercury*, which contains articles, photographs and family histories. Many of these were researched and written by well-known fairground historians.

Of particular use and interest to family history researchers is the large collection of photographs of fair folk and fair rides. Whilst many of the photos featuring fair people do not give names, they do give a real flavour of life in a caravan, the type of clothing fair folk wore at the given date, and the size of family groups. There are over 80,000 photographs in the collections at the archive and archive staff have begun the immense task of digitalizing these. Many of the photographs were donated by fairground families and depict people, rides and places that would otherwise have been forgotten. The online image database at www.shef.ac.uk/nfa currently contains over 1,000 photographic images. A search and find feature on the website allows you to request images by region, category, ride owner, location and act.

The Mitchell and Kenyon collection is important to anyone interested in the history of early film. It involves collaboration between the National Fairground Archive and the British Film Institute to study hundreds of non-fiction films commissioned by showmen in the first decade of the twentieth century.

For those unable to visit the archive in person, the website is particularly detailed and provides plenty of information and images relating to the history of fairs. It is an excellent starting point, especially if you are looking for information about which fairs visited a particular locality, or about the people who worked for a particular fair. The various sideshows and novelties that made up the travelling fair are also described on the website. These include the popular boxing booths that operated until the 1960s, freak shows and rides ranging from the steam-powered roundabouts of the 1860s to the American novelty rides that arrived in this country after the Second World War.

YORKSHIRE FILM ARCHIVE

Based at York St John College, the Yorkshire Film Archive deals with one of the most modern types of archive discussed in this book: the moving image. The Yorkshire Film Archive seeks to find and preserve and provide access to over a century's worth of moving images about all aspects of life in Yorkshire.

Yorkshire is believed to be the first place in the world where a moving image was captured on film and the film archive holds these images, which are of Leeds bridge and were recorded by film pioneer Louis le Prince in 1888.

The films which have been preserved cover a wide range of subjects and the archive documents life during the last century, through to the present day, in a way that no other medium can. The archive has recently developed the Yorkshire Video Collection, which comprises documentary films depicting life, leisure and education in Yorkshire between 1998 and 2001. One of the highlights of the collection, and one which will no doubt be of fascination to future family history researchers, is the film *Saying their Prayers* (2000) which records the different ways Yorkshire people of various religions worship.

The archive's collections are particularly strong on the industries which made Yorkshire famous throughout the world, including steel manufacture, mining and textiles. Agriculture is also well featured and the archives include footage of hay making and dairy farming in North Yorkshire. One particularly interesting fact about the agriculture film footage is that some of the films show the same subject, for example hay making, more than once, but for different decades, giving the viewer the chance to see how the process changed and developed over the years.

As well as these various jobs and industries, there is plenty of film about leisure and home life. One of the most interesting leisure films the archives holds is the programme *Rachel Discovers the Sea*, a 1936 family film about a simple seaside holiday, showing what leisure activities our ancestors would have enjoyed before the Second World War. There is also film footage designed to show the area as a tourist destination, with features about Scarborough and York and the tourist facilities they offered visitors at different times during the twentieth century.

One of the largest collections in the archive is from the amateur film maker Charles Chislett of Rotherham. Chislett shot over 100 films between 1935 and 1960. Many of these featured his own family life and the films include footage of his trip on the maiden voyage of the *Queen Mary* liner. Finally, perhaps one of the most unusual films is that of the Wakefield and Castlefield Marbles Championship, recorded in 1933, showing one of the most harmless pastimes our ancestors might have enjoyed.

The Yorkshire Film Archive is open to researchers by appointment only and features a viewing room which has facilities for up to five researchers at a time. Many of us regularly make videos of our own family activities, perhaps with an eye to our descendants enjoying finding out what our own lives were like. Specialist staff at the archive are able to offer advice about the storage and preservation of moving images, so that our own memories can be treasured by future generations.

Chapter 6

RELIGION: ESTABLISHED CHURCH AND NONCONFORMITY

People from all over the world have made their home in Yorkshire and this is reflected in the number of different religions represented in the region. Religion has historically been a flashpoint in various communities and Yorkshire is no exception. From the arrival of thousands of Irish Roman Catholic immigrants into towns and villages that were hostile to Catholicism to more recent conflicts involving Asian religions, local newspapers have been keen to record outbreaks of intolerance and even violence.

One of the earliest instances of religious persecution in Yorkshire was the twelfth-century massacre of Jews in York. In 1190, a mob of jealous citizens attacked a group of Jews, who fled to the city's castle. Some of the Jews killed themselves and the rest were murdered by the angry mob. A list of the debts that non-Jews owed the Jews was burned by those who had attacked the group.

Roman Catholic records are particularly well represented in Yorkshire, dating from the years when it was illegal to hold a Catholic service in England through to the arrival of Irish immigrants who settled in large groups in the region's towns and cities during Victorian times, provoking complaints from the local population.

There are many aspects of searching for ancestors through religious records that are common to the whole of the UK. But Yorkshire can be different in some respects. First, North Yorkshire had a very strong Roman Catholic tradition, particularly during the years when practising Catholicism was illegal, even at times when the religion had died in most other areas of the country.

The county also has the benefit of being the home of the York Minster Archives, one of the most important holdings for religious records in the whole

Yorkshire is home to many different religions.

country and of the Borthwick Institute, which specializes in ecclesiastical history. We will learn more about how these and other archives can help in researching the religions of our ancestors in this chapter.

Some places of worship have preferred to keep their own records, rather than submitting them to central record offices. But it is often fairly easy to find out where particular religious records are housed and to make an appointment to see them.

Records for non-Christian faiths, such as Islam or Judaism, can be particularly challenging to the family history researcher, as many of these are written in a foreign language. Some of these religious archives are still kept by the relevant place of worship. It is usually possible to make an appointment to view these and help may be available with any difficulties encountered due to language. From the mid-nineteenth century, many municipal cemeteries also had sections for non-Christian burials. These are usually in a separate section of the burial ground. The archive office nearest to the place where your ancestors lived should be able to advise where non-Christian religious records are kept and even point you in the right direction for help and advice on dealing with these documents.

THE ORGANIZATION OF RELIGIOUS RECORDS

Because many religious groups have faced hostility or persecution at some point in their history, their records and archives have not always survived or were perhaps not even kept in the first place. The Hardwick Act of 1754 stated that everyone except Jews and Quakers had to be married in the established church or face transportation from the country.

Understandably, such a stiff penalty meant that those who wished to go through a marriage ceremony for their own religion would not want a record of the occasion to be kept for posterity. Many people opted to marry in both their own religion and go through a Church of England ceremony for the sake of keeping to the law. This means that if you find a marriage of your ancestors in a Church of England parish register before 1837, it is not safe to assume that they followed the beliefs of the established church.

The Hardwick Act was repealed by the Civil Registration Act of 1837. This Act, as well as beginning the central recording of births, marriages and deaths, meant that religions other than the Church of England, Jewish or Quaker faiths were also authorized to conduct and register their own marriage ceremonies on premises that had been registered beforehand, where a registrar was present at the ceremony. All religious communities could now keep their own records without fear of legal reprisals. Those religious records dealing with

Records relating to the established church are easiest to access (Adel Parish Church).

birth, marriage and death would, following the Civil Registration Act, be duplicated by official records now kept centrally.

THE ESTABLISHED CHURCH

Records relating to the Church of England are the easiest to access, simply because the religion has been the official one of the country for hundreds of years and so has been adhered to by most people, albeit sometimes in name only. An important Act which has determined where we can find Church of England records was the 1978 Church of England Parochial Registers and Records Measure. This facilitated and encouraged the passing of Church of England parish records and registers to local record offices. Each diocese (group of parishes) would designate one or more record office which would serve its churches, and all records over 100 years old that were not still in use were to be deposited at that record office. A phone call to the nearest record office to the church serving the area where an ancestor lived is usually all that is needed to determine where the parish records for that place of worship are deposited.

The parish is the basic unit of church administration. Most Yorkshire

Many Yorkshire parishes were established by the seventeenth century. Denton Parish Church has Anglo-Saxon origins.

parishes were established by the seventeenth century, but some were created during the industrial boom of the nineteenth century. At this time new churches were created to cater for the growing number of people arriving to take jobs in the region.

In some cases original parish registers were lost or damaged over the years and so were not able to be deposited at a record office. This does not mean, though, that all the information the registers would have contained has been lost. There may be copies of the records in Bishops' Transcripts. This system, in use from 1598 until the end of the nineteenth century, meant that every year ministers were required to copy all entries of births, marriages and deaths that had taken place at their church that year and pass the copy to the bishop, to be stored separately. The success of the system partly depended on the diligence of the individual minister and of the bishop and his clerks in chasing late or missing records, but the transcripts can be invaluable where original records are unobtainable.

The Borthwick Institute of Historical Research in York holds most of the records for Yorkshire Church of England parishes, with those for the arch-deaconry of Richmond held at West Yorkshire Archive Service, Leeds.

NONCONFORMITY

There are various different forms of religious dissent, but anyone who was classed as a Nonconformist practised a different type of religion to the established church of the time. Nonconformity has both positive and negative points from a family history research point of view.

It can be positive because many dissenting groups, such as the Quakers, kept extremely meticulous and detailed records, many of which can still be viewed today. It can be negative where, as religious dissent was either frowned upon, not socially acceptable or even illegal, threat of persecution or arrest mean that religious records relating to the group were not kept or have not survived.

Books of dissenter baptisms exist from the mid-seventeenth century onwards, but their existence is patchy because of risk of discovery by the authorities. Roman Catholic registers begin from the eighteenth century.

ROMAN CATHOLICISM

Roman Catholic ancestors can be difficult to trace through religious records as there have been times when Roman Catholics were outlawed or unwelcome in Yorkshire and the rest of the UK. Even when Catholicism was tolerated, there was often hatred against members of the religion who lived in the county. This occurred in cases such as the aftermath of the Irish potato famine of 1845, when thousands of Irish people, many of whom were Roman Catholics, left their native land and sailed to Liverpool in order to seek employment in Yorkshire's large towns.

When King Henry VIII broke with the Pope in 1531, England was proclaimed to be no longer a Roman Catholic country and the population were expected to convert to the Church of England. However, it was not until 1559 that it was actually illegal to hold or attend a Roman Catholic service in England. The defeat of the Spanish Armada in 1588 thwarted an attempt by Spain to overthrow England's anointed monarch and restore the Roman Catholic religion to the country. For this reason, those who practised the 'old religion', i.e. Catholicism, were forced to keep their faith a secret.

Obviously, anyone attempting to keep records of any aspect of Catholic life during this period would have been risking their lives, so records are scarce. Official records of those who persisted in Catholicism dating back to the reign of Queen Elizabeth I (1558–1603) are particularly revealing, as they show how Catholicism flourished in North Yorkshire at a time when it was snuffed out elsewhere in the country.

Documents held at the North Yorkshire County Record Office at Northallerton build a picture of how the religion was able to flourish in this area. These documents include memoirs and biographies of local gentry,

Myddleton Lodge, near Ilkley, was one of the places Roman Catholic priests were given shelter from the authorities.

volumes of the Catholic Record Society and lists of recusants for the North Riding.

At the time that Catholicism was forbidden, Catholic priests were educated and ordained abroad and then returned to England to minister to Catholics in secret. The only way they were able to do this was with the cooperation of local families. These were usually people of means, with the political power to keep their activities secret.

Grosmont Farm, on the North Yorkshire moors, was one such stronghold, where priests were given shelter and sent out to minister to the local population with clothing and money provided by gentry families. North Yorkshire is particularly noted as an area of strong Catholicism during the sixteenth century for both rich and poor people. This makes this area of the county markedly different to most other areas of England at this time. Catholicism was restricted to mainly wealthy people during the time it was banned, but the North Riding list of recusants, which quotes the occupations of those mentioned, shows people of all social classes, including those engaged in manual labour or farm work. Whitby was another hotbed for receiving priests from overseas, and anyone helping Catholic clergy was fined or had possessions taken from them.

Catholics who did not conform with the law and continued to worship following their own religion would be prosecuted at quarter sessions. The majority of quarter session records are held at local and county record offices. Most people would have been fined for not attending Church of England services, with punishments such as imprisonment being reserved for only the most serious and persistent cases. Whatever the punishment, quarter sessions records often contain the names of those who had been prosecuted for non-attendance at church, particularly during the sixteenth and seventeenth centuries.

The ban on Catholicism lasted until 1778, when the Emancipation Act was brought in and laws of persecution against Catholic priests were repealed, meaning Catholics were once again able to buy and inherit land. Thirteen years later, Catholics were again allowed to attend or say the Mass and it was no longer against the law to be a priest.

By the time it was again legal to be a Catholic in England, more formal records were kept along similar lines to those of the established church. Some have now been deposited in Yorkshire county record offices. A call to the main record office of a particular Yorkshire region (see directory in Chapter 10) will establish whether the records of a church your ancestor may have attended are kept there. If they are not in the keeping of the record office, staff can usually help you to find out where they are.

Many Roman Catholic registers are still with parish priests or in diocesan archives. Before 1850, the country was administered by Vicars Apostolic, who presided over large areas. The Bishop of Leeds holds some of the records of the Northern Vicariate.

A friendly local priest who presides over a parish in which you have a particular interest may be able to help out. However, it is down to the goodwill of the individual and to what records are actually held as to how helpful you may find them. Some priests, particularly those who minister to older churches built during Victorian times, may have extensive collections of church material that could prove invaluable.

Collections could include copies of parish magazines (listing social events, prizegivings and religious ceremonies), the records of Catholic societies such as the Society of St Vincent de Paul (which did good works locally and arranged social events for all ages), as well as old photographs and written records of the church's history. Similarly, orders of brothers and nuns may have extensive and interesting archives, which they may allow an interested researcher to view by appointment.

Where records of Roman Catholic baptisms exist, they are extremely useful to the researcher, as they usually detail the names of godparents, who tended to be friends or relations of the baby's parents. Along with the expected records of births, marriages and deaths you may find registers of confirmations. Nowadays, Catholic children are confirmed at secondary school age. During the nineteenth century, confirmation was more likely to take place between the ages of 7 and 9. A confirmation register will give the first and surname of each child, together with the confirmation name they had chosen.

Luckily for researchers, from the twentieth century onwards, the Catholic system of organization of parishes was very similar to that of the established church. Areas were divided into parishes, each cared for by a priest and a group of parishes was (and still is) called a diocese, presided over by a bishop. Before this time, things were less organized and priests tended to travel over wide areas and minister to the populations as and when needed.

The North West Catholic History Society, based in Wigan, has published the records of Bishop John Leyburn, which could be extremely useful to anyone researching Catholic ancestors in the north of England. Bishop Leyburn travelled much of the north of England in 1687, and his mission was to confirm as many Catholics as possible. He actually confirmed 20,000 people, who have been listed by the North West Catholic History Society.

The Emancipation Act did not mean an end to the persecution of Catholics, particularly when those Catholics were people who had come to Yorkshire from overseas. At times of high immigration, such as the Industrial Revolution, some Yorkshire people were against Irish immigrants, accusing them of introducing papist ways into England and of taking jobs that would otherwise have gone to native Yorkshire people. Accounts of the foundation of St Patrick's Church in 1852 in Bradford show how easily hostility could arise. Irish people of the Bradford area had saved for several years to build a second church in the town for the local Catholic community. A ceremony to mark the laying of the foundation stone on St Patrick's Day (17 March) 1852 was marred by protests by people who were opposed to the presence of a Roman Catholic group in the area.

Records and Reminiscences of St Patrick's Church, Bradford was written by Fr John Earnshaw and is held at Bradford Local Studies Library. The author discussed the feelings of those who were taking part in the foundation ceremony of St Patrick's Church and revealed that they had several fears before the dedication service. According to Fr Earnshaw, the congregation of the new church felt that it would not be wise to parade in the streets with a St Patrick's banner and a crucifix, as was usual when an event such as the opening of a church was being celebrated, so they decided to proceed quietly to the church without bringing themselves and their cause to the attention of the local non-Catholic population. Nevertheless, several thousand people attended the laying of the foundation stone and Earnshaw described the scene as crowds milled around watching the ceremony:

> During the proceedings, an occasional crash was heard, followed by a shriek, indicative that some barrier had given way or that the roof of some frail shed overweighed had fallen in.

The opening of the church was so important that it was featured in the *Bradford Observer* newspaper. The paper reported that a solemn high Mass was celebrated by the Bishop of Beverley, attended by a number of priests from other Catholic churches in the area. The church, said the article, had cost around £4,000 to build, of which only half had so far been raised. Despite the ill-feeling that accompanied its foundation, St Patrick's managed to attract and maintain a loyal congregation and recently celebrated its 150th anniversary.

OTHER NONCONFORMITY

The nineteenth century was a boom period to people who wished to worship outside the established church. It is during this time that religions such as Methodism, Quakers and Baptists flourished and gained huge numbers of recruits from the Church of England. Unlike Catholicism, because there was no persecution involved, most religious records for these religions have been kept, have survived and are now lodged in county record offices.

As we saw in the Roman Catholic section of this chapter, the officiating minister of a church or chapel may still sometimes be keeper of a valuable set of archives. What has survived will vary from area to area, but it is always worth enquiring about archives at an existing place of worship if you think an ancestor may have attended. If they were actively involved in church social life, there could be photographs or reports about them.

METHODISM

Methodism became strong in Yorkshire after the county was included on several of the preaching tours Methodism founder John Wesley made in the years after 1738. Methodism is particularly different to the Church of England because Methodist churches are organized into circuits rather than parishes.

Methodist registers begin around the 1790s, but they can be difficult to work with as the system of circuits where preachers visited different towns and villages in their area of responsibility changed so often. It is necessary to know which circuit the town or village you are researching fell under at the time you are looking for. This is an area where the experience and knowledge of local record office staff can be invaluable. Members of the family history society for a particular area may also be able to help with queries about circuit areas.

It was Nonconformists who played a big part in making the provision for registry offices to record births, marriages and deaths through the Civil Registration Act of 1837. As we have seen, the Act meant that no one was obliged to attend a Church of England religious ceremony in order to make their marriage legal. Weddings could take place at registered Nonconformist churches or chapels and be perfectly legal.

THE RELIGIOUS SOCIETY OF FRIENDS (QUAKERS)

The Religious Society of Friends, or Quakers, as they are more commonly known, was established in the East Midlands during the 1640s. The religion was embraced throughout the country by the end of 1640s. Quakerism stressed equality for all and although many Quakers were persecuted for following their religion and, in doing so, refusing to comply with the law, the peaceful and non-confrontational nature of the Quaker faith meant that few people were openly hostile to the religion.

Anyone with Quaker ancestors can be pleased that, because of the meticulous record keeping of the Society, there are many more Quaker records in Yorkshire's archives than exist for those of other Nonconformist groups such as Baptists and Independents.

Quaker records of births, marriages and deaths exist in the same places as other Nonconformist religious records, but Quaker marriage records contain extra information for the family historian. It was the custom at a Quaker marriage for everyone present at the ceremony to sign the marriage register. This gives the researcher the extra bonus of knowing which friends and family attended the happy event.

The Quaker system of administration was through a system of meetings, at which minutes were kept. The minutes of these meetings can be invaluable to the genealogist. The first tier of meeting was the preparative meeting, at which material was prepared for a monthly meeting. Both these levels of meetings dealt with matters within the Quaker community such as disciplinary issues, membership of the Society, finances and property disputes. Quakers could be disowned from the Society of Friends for offences such as persistently missing meetings, condoning war (war was against the beliefs of the religion) and fornication before marriage.

The next level of meeting was the Quarterly meeting, which received representatives from the monthly meetings. These Quarterly meetings in turn sent representatives to the Yearly meeting, which was held in London. The minutes of this highest level of meeting are available at Friends House Library in London, but contain little of interest to anyone tracing a Yorkshire Quaker ancestor.

Many local record offices hold copies of the minutes of local monthly meetings. The records of the Richmond Monthly Meeting of the Religious Society of Friends are held at North Yorkshire County Record Office and provide a good example of the type of material a researcher can expect to call upon when tracing a Quaker ancestor in Yorkshire. The records of the monthly meetings for the Richmond area, which covered a large district, including parts of Swaledale and Wensleydale, cover the years between 1673 and 1934. Wensleydale seems to have been a particularly fertile ground for the Quaker religion. Many of the Friends in this area became prosperous and gained a good social standing and among their members was the physician William Hillary (1697–1763).

The peaceable nature of the religion is shown in the fact that any disagreement between members was always called a 'difference' rather than an argument or dispute. The Richmond records of 1716 report an interesting scandal, which must have caused some 'difference' between Society members, when certain of the Quaker numbers were spotted at a race meeting on Middleham Moor, going against the Quaker beliefs of avoiding all gambling.

Perhaps some of the most evocative documents that survive in the North Yorkshire County Record Office are the Records of Friends' Sufferings, or Great Books of Sufferings, as they are sometimes known. These papers, dating from 1659 to 1856, document the clashes that Quakers had with those outside their religion. The amount of detail which is often given is a fascinating record of a time when to follow the Quaker religion was to continually be at odds with the rest of society. Many of the 'sufferings' recorded in these documents came about because the Quakers did not believe in the payment of tithes or church rates. The authorities, when faced with a refusal to pay, would often simply seize personal goods to the value of the tax owed, and the results of the seizing were documented in the Records of Sufferings. For example, in 1671, one young woman was left 'neither stocke no stocking but what she had on', following a raid by the authorities. The books record that many Quaker members were sent to prison because of their refusal to pay tithes.

One of the leading Quaker families in the Wensleydale area were the

Robinsons of Countersett Hall. Richard Robinson began Quaker meetings at the hall in 1650 and was soon at odds with neighbouring Bartholomew Herison who was apparently 'subject to take a sup of drinke and then letting his tongue clatter to the dishonour of God'. The records tell that meetings were not to be held at Herison's house until matters improved.

The Quaker Collection

Yorkshire is home to one of the largest Quaker record repositories outside London: the Quaker Collection at the Special Collections department of Leeds University library. The collection comprises two main sections: first, the Carlton Hill and Clifford Street collections, original documentary archives relating to parts of West and North Yorkshire and York and Thirsk areas respectively. The second section is made up of photocopied and microfilmed sets of various Quaker birth, marriage and death certificates.

The Carlton Hill and Clifford Street collections can seem quite confusing to use because of the fact that the catchment area for the four levels of Quaker meetings changed over time. The documents include minute books and lists of members and each item has its own reference number. Indexes are available to help researchers find the required item.

The lists of members held in the Quaker collection can be extremely useful because of the detailed information they contain. When searching for an individual or family, it is important to remember that, because the catchment areas for meetings could be very wide, an individual may not have attended a meeting in the town where they lived.

Where a member is listed, there is often the added bonus of finding other family members listed alongside. The details given usually include the member's name, the names of their parents, their occupation, address and (if applicable) when and why they left a meeting area, for example, death or moving to another location.

Yorkshire Quaker Heritage Project

The Yorkshire Quaker Heritage Project is a developing online source of information about the location of Quaker archives and records in Yorkshire (defined by the pre-1974 county boundaries) and archives outside the county that are of Yorkshire interest.

The website (www.hull.ac.uk/oldlib/archives/quaker/locreg.htm) allows the user to search for Quaker records in a variety of ways. These include searching by town or village name, the name of an individual, the name of a Quaker meeting, a type of collection or a particular archive repository.

A search under the place name 'Ilkley' brought up four records, which included records for families including the Andrews of Askwith and the Horsfalls of Leeds; records of Ilkley Preparative meetings from 1862 to date;

1960s records for Ilkley Young Friends group and records of the Ilkley branch of the Missionary Helpers Union. All of these records were listed as being held at Leeds University Library and the relevant index numbers are given, which can be quoted at the library when requesting the material.

Around 450 collections are listed on the database, which is regularly updated. Because work is still ongoing on the website, some searches may bring up very limited results. Nevertheless, the site is an important and useful way of finding Quaker records from one source and an excellent starting point for research on Quaker ancestors.

THE BORTHWICK INSTITUTE OF HISTORICAL RESEARCH, YORK

The Borthwick is one of the biggest archives outside London and has been established for over 50 years. Its archives are housed in purpose-built accommodation at the University of York. The Borthwick Institute is an extremely important archive for anyone hoping to trace an ancestor through religious records, as the archive specializes in ecclesiastical records.

For the purposes of ecclesiastical administration, England is divided into two units: the provinces of Canterbury and York, each presided over by an archbishop. The Borthwick holds parish records for the archdeaconry of York and records of the province and diocese of York.

The institute also holds most of the parish register transcripts for the diocese of York from 1600 onwards. These were also known as bishops' transcripts which, as we saw earlier in this chapter, are copies of parish registers which were sent to the diocesan authority, ideally on a once-yearly basis.

One of the major holdings of use to family historians are the thousands of probate records. These deal with arrangements for the distribution of property after a person's death. Probate records can include wills, inventories and administration bonds. Most of the probate registers are on microfilm. If a will was proved before January 1858 and falls under the diocese of York, it should be at the Borthwick. The only exception is the diocese of Chester.

Other records held at the Borthwick relate to what can be the most interesting type of research, records from when things went wrong. The institute holds several records for Catholic Apostolic Churches in the West Yorkshire area for the late nineteenth century. Among the papers are details of those who refused pastoral care, 'persons unfaithful' and also a book of regulations for saying Mass and carrying out various services. This collection is explored further in the case study at the end of this chapter.

There is also a separate collection of relinquishment of orders, which is what happened when a priest or deacon wished to leave his position within the church. The Clerical Disabilities Act of 1870 made provision for a religious pastor to execute a deed of relinquishment of office. The Borthwick holds a collection of office copies of these deeds, from 1870 to 1896, as well as correspondence relating to the matters brought up by the resignations.

THE CHURCH LADS' AND CHURCH GIRLS' BRIGADE

The Church Lads' and Church Girls' Brigade were one of the most popular 'brigade' organizations which provided a social life outside school for thousands of youngsters from the 1890s onwards.

The Brigade was founded over 100 years ago, at a time when many members of society were concerned about the physical and spiritual welfare of young people. Most children left school at the age of 13 and often went into hard physical work, with little time for leisure or socializing. The brigades were set up to give those youngsters the chance to form friendships and gain confidence in a friendly Christian environment.

Brigades such as the Church Lads' were popular both with the church and government. The church was in favour of them because brigade attendance at church parades kept young people at religious services and the government liked the idea of having military cadets to call upon on in times of need.

The Church Lads' and Church Girls' Brigade headquarters are at Wath Upon Dearne, near Sheffield, where researchers are welcome to visit the archives by prior appointment. Although there are no details of individual brigade members, the archives hold file cards detailing each Church Lads' Brigade company that has existed throughout the world from 1891 to c.1980. The cards give details of church connections for each company and dates of company formation.

Staff are usually able to give information about medals or badges that researchers would like identifying, which may have been passed down through the family from an ancestor who was a brigade member. They can usually help identify either the items themselves, or a photograph of the medal or badge.

Many researchers come forward with badges or medals which were awarded to a family member, hoping to find out more about the meaning of the award. The Brigade had badges and medals for hundreds of different events and activities. Medals were awarded for attendance and cloth or metal badges were presented upon successful completion of activities such as bugling, drumming and camping. Fob badges were given for sports and competitions. There were various different ranks in the Church Lads' Brigade, from private (lad) to colonel (officer).

The Brigade, founded by Walter Mallock Gee in 1891, has a history of military involvement, which was particularly helpful during the First and Second World Wars. When the government issued a call to arms in 1914, the 16th Battalion King's Royal Rifle Corps was formed, made up entirely of current and former Church Lad's members. The battalion suffered heavy losses at the Somme battlefield.

The sacrifice made by Church Lads' members was recognized when the Brigade presented a banner of its patron saint Martin of Tours at Westminster Abbey in November 1921. The dedication service was attended by around 3,000 brigade members, officers and war veterans. The Brigade went on to make valuable contributions to the war effort during the Second World War when members too young to volunteer for active service helped their communities by carrying out tasks such as guarding reservoirs and sounding the all-clear bugle after an air raid.

Girls were not left out of the Brigade movement and the Church, Nursing and Ambulance Brigade for Young Women and Girls was founded in 1901. Seven years later, the Brigade movements could boast 70,000 male and 8,000 female members in the UK. Both girls and boys took part in sporting and charitable challenges as the twentieth century progressed, with the Brigade being one of the first in the UK to participate in the Duke of Edinburgh Award Scheme. A National Band was formed in 1979 and the Brigade now offers membership to young people between the ages of 5 and 21. It must be one of the few organizations for young people that has lasted more than 100 years.

CHURCHYARDS AND BURIAL GROUNDS

If you wish to see, or search for an ancestor's grave, or a family vault, most burials before the 1800s will have been in the parish church graveyard of the person's home town. Dissenters did not generally have their own burial grounds.

The rapid growth of towns such as Sheffield and Bradford during the Industrial Revolution was one of the reasons for an Act of Parliament in 1853 which made provision for local authorities to create new non-denominational cemeteries. Many of these new cemeteries had separate sections for Anglican and dissenter burials, with most featuring a west end for Church of England burials and space for Nonconformist burials at the east end of the sites.

One of the finest examples of a public cemetery is Bradford's Undercliffe cemetery, which contains six listed monuments. Victorian cemeteries such as Undercliffe were seen as public amenities and places of leisure. Undercliffe is one of the most striking cemeteries of this era, with its wide walkways and the spectacular view of the city at the end of the cemetery's grand central promenade.

Competition was fierce for a place on this promenade, with people reserving their places for after death. Land agent Joseph Smith got arguably the best plot in the cemetery as a perk of his job. It was written into his employment contract when he worked at Undercliffe that he would occupy a plot at the very end of

Undercliffe cemetery contains six listed monuments.

Many tombstones tell a story through their inscriptions.

The Behrens family mausoleum at
Undercliffe cemetery, Bradford.

the promenade upon his death. His obelisk memorial is still visible from Bradford city centre.

It can be very enjoyable to wander around a cemetery or graveyard looking for an ancestor's grave. But on a huge site such as Undercliffe, where there have been over 120,000 interments, it could take weeks of searching to find the correct burial plot. Most cemetery records are held at the record office of the town or city concerned. Those for Undercliffe are held at Bradford archives, which have burial registers from the cemetery's opening in 1854 through to 1958. If the local record office does not hold the registers of a particular burial ground, they should be able to advise where these are located.

Local studies libraries and family history societies also often hold transcribed records of gravestones in their locality. These are usually indexed and can be particularly useful where it has become difficult to read the carving on an actual memorial stone, or where the gravestone itself is inaccessible, or no longer in situ.

If you do manage to find the memorial of one of your ancestors, or even a family grave, the inscription on the stone is only part of the story. As we shall see, there are many other clues about a person's life to be found on a single gravestone. It is of immense value to be able to read when the person concerned died and how old they were. Many inscriptions also detail other family members or give other information about the life of the deceased.

The following two examples, taken from Wortley Cemetery, West Yorkshire, show how the amount of information given on a memorial stone can vary greatly. The first example of an inscription gave a minimum amount of detail:

In memory of Matthew Bevison of the late Benjamin and Mary Bevison. He died on the 8th of June 1834, aged 36 years.

The second inscription went into much more detail, not only giving information about the life of the deceased, but plenty of useful facts about the family:

> Beneath this stone are interred the remains of Ann the wife of James Bateson of Highfield House in this town. She died June 10th AD 1834 aged 66 years.
>
> Also Matilda Caroline, youngest daughter of the above James and Ann Bateston and wife of John Burkhill, corn-merchant of Louth, Lincs. She died on March 13th AD 1838 aged 29 years. Also the above named James Bateson who died April 3rd AD 1848 aged 75 years. He was a liberal benefactor to this church and also one of the original trustees of Advowson. Also of Hannah Bateston, wife of the above-named James Bateston who also died December 18th AD 1866 aged 79 years.

Perhaps because the second example is a family grave, rather than a single interment, it gives more information about those who are buried there. But it shows clearly how much information can be gleaned from a gravestone.

However, particularly for Victorian graves, the images carved on to the stone, or the statues incorporated into the monument, were carefully chosen to be symbolic and can give further clues to supplement your research. For example, clasped hands indicate that a husband and wife have been united in death, a broken column symbolizes the end of the male line and a scythe can indicate that someone was cut down in the prime of life, often in tragic circumstances.

It was also the fashion during the nineteenth century for gravestones of tradespeople to be decorated with symbols which related to their profession. Thus, Undercliffe cemetery is home to the grave of a vet, complete with a carving of the coat of arms of the Royal College of Veterinary Surgeons, a pestle and mortar decorate the grave of an apothecary and a keen cricketer's final resting place has a bat and ball on the gravestone.

Church graveyards tend to hold more traditional memorial stones, but can also provide more clues about the deceased. Families or individuals who possessed wealth or standing in their community usually had larger memorials than the rest of the population and their graves were often in more noticeable locations, around the main pathways or at the east end of the church exterior. A search through a parish churchyard may also reveal several tombstones for the same surname, offering the possibility that all those people were related.

CASE STUDY: THE RECORDS OF THE CATHOLIC APOSTOLIC CHURCH, HORTON, BRADFORD

These records are held at the Borthwick Institute, at the University of York. The Catholic Apostolic Church was an international movement which reached Britain in 1835. Although the movement took inspiration from the Roman Catholic Church for some of its rituals and services, it was a separate religious community. The Catholic Apostolic brethren were convinced of the imminent second coming and were only prepared to ordain one set of church officials, believing that by the time all those officials had died, the world would have ended. When the religion's last official died in 1971, all ministrations ceased with immediate effect.

These church records are a good case study as they demonstrate the broad base of religious records that can exist for a single church and also show how these records can be used in our own research. They are very detailed, mentioning hundreds of people by name and provide plenty of information for background research. One of the most useful of the records in this collection is the *General Rubrics and Book of Regulations*, which was published in London in 1878 and acted as a handbook for the church pastor. It contained a wide variety of prayers for situations from childbirth to penitence, from dealing with a pastor's leave of absence to music to be used in church services. Alongside the prayers were instructions as to how the pastor should behave in certain situations and, even more fascinating, how he should preserve and treat official documents and church property.

The whole set of records of this particular church has one continuous message: that those who did not practise the faith regularly would be removed from the church's care. The rubric's instructions for praying for a woman and child after childbirth stated that 'this office should only be used in cases where the mother or father has been received under the pastoral care of the church'. The rubric went on to state that a private baptism was only to be used where the infant was in danger of imminent death. If the infant recovered, it was to be brought into church by its sponsors for an official baptism ceremony. The water used in the baptism was to be pure and fresh each time and was not to be thrown down a 'common drain'.

The book of rubrics contained in this collection had certainly been read by its owner as there are handwritten notes in the margin every few pages with small amendments or comments. The strictness of the church is shown in the instructions as to how to treat those who had not taken holy communion for a long time. They were to be, instructs the book, 'brought to a sense of guilt and made to seek absolution before continuing'.

Similar instructions reveal the church's attitude towards those who were joining the faith and are a good indication of how any of our ancestors who joined the Catholic Apostolic Church would have been treated. The book advises that a deacon of the church should visit the person or family who would be joining the faith, instruct them as to where they could find seats in church and advise when prayer meetings took place. If the newly admitted people had no friends in the faith, the deacon was to introduce them to 'faithful and discreet persons in their own rank in life'.

The rule book contained a list of forbidden marriages, which were also to be displayed in the church vestry. Among the forbidden unions was a man marrying his mother's sister or his father's brother's wife, or a woman marrying her grandmother's husband or her son's son.

The next section of the book relates to the keeping and preservation of the church's records. There is a list of records which the pastor was expected to keep within the church. The fact that most of these still exist in this particular collection is testament to the diligence of the pastors of this particular church, at least. The list included registers of baptism and marriage, of regular and occasional communicants and 'lapsed persons' who had rejected pastoral care. Records were to be kept of those who helped in the church, including deacons and lay assistants, and the pastor was to ensure that council minutes and records connected to the history of the church were safely preserved. If only every church and chapel had begun and kept such extensive records, our own family history research would be much easier. A final word of warning in the book reminded the pastor that the records were the property of the church and were to be left with the church, whatever should become of him.

There are several registers of baptisms in the Catholic Apostolic Church of Horton collection at the Borthwick Institute. As well as listing the names of the child that had been baptized, both parents were listed, with the mother's maiden name noted alongside the family's address. Both the date of birth and that date of the baby's baptism were listed, as well as the names and signatures of the sponsors, who were not always family members.

It is interesting to see how long after birth the baptisms took place. One of the entries is for the Riley family, who had several children baptized at once in February 1877, presumably after converting to the Apostolic Church. The parents of the family were William Riley and Betty (nee Ambler) who lived at St Andrew's Place, Bradford. The children baptized at the ceremony were Walter, aged 15, Edward aged 13, Frances Mary Jane aged 11, Amy aged 6 and Mabel aged 2.

As with many family history records, it is the more unusual entries on a document that can bring it to life. Another baptism entry in the same book, this time for an Edward Farrer, shows how disputes could occur in a family over religious practices. Edward was baptized in November 1877 and the remarks at the end of the entry stated that he died the same day. The pastor had written: 'the father having refused to allow any minister to baptize the child and death being imminent the rite was administered by a lay member at the request of the mother'.

Lay members seem to have been a big part of life at this church, with a register recording the details of lay assistants. The listings give a good idea not only of what type of work lay people could undertake, but also indicate how long they carried out their duties, and the reasons they left. Elizabeth Simpson is listed as being a lay assistant in the capacity of singer. She resigned from her duties in December 1880, citing the pressures of being married and having young children. Among the other duties listed for lay members in the same register were instructing children and visiting the sick.

The register also included lists of priests, giving the date of their call to the office of priest, their ordination and, if applicable, when they were moved to another church. The register of deacons and deaconesses follows a similar pattern, and gave the addresses of these officers, who lived in their own homes, visiting the church to carry out their duties.

The register of 'persons unfaithful' is one of three similar registers kept by the Apostolic Church; the other two being register of regular communicants and of infrequent communicants. All of these lists include the names of the people concerned, often with comments in the 'remarks' section. One such remark concerned a Henry Walton who was added to the 'persons unfaithful' list on 5 October 1903. The remarks section stated that he was found drowned on 30 December 1904.

Not all comments contain such drama, but they do have useful information, such as details of when a person had moved to another parish or had been married. Occupations were also often listed, giving a good idea not only of an ancestor's work but of the social makeup of the congregation. A few of the entries also included information about some of the younger church-goers being adopted, and who was caring for them.

The list of regular communicants runs to over 1,000 over a ten-year period, with some members eventually being transferred to the register of those departed in the faith. This register gives the name of the departed, their date of death, whether they had been anointed before death and the cause of their demise. The detail in the causes of death varies: John William Shackleton died in February 1900, in war in South Africa, whereas Eliza Gane died 'rather suddenly' in April 1879.

The causes of death, when seen in a register which covers a period of several years, can be a useful barometer of local and even national events. Several entries may occur together, such as deaths by smallpox, or during wartime, showing problems that were affecting a community at a particular time.

The register of those 'who having been communicants reject or decline the pastoral care of the faith' is fascinating. An entry for Donald McCallum Sproul for March 1876 is particularly strongly worded: 'the apostle decides that Mr Sproul is a person of ungodly life, utterly unworthy of being among the communicants of the church'. The entry actually throws up more questions about Mr Sproul's behaviour than it answers, but it is a glimpse into the church's attitudes towards those who didn't keep to the rules. Arthur Vanham was listed in June 1891 because he had married the sister of his dead wife at Bradford Parish Church, where presumably such a union was not outlawed.

Similarly, John Edwin Hainsworth entered the register in July 1902 for becoming a Roman Catholic. The church, though, did show some compassion towards those fallen in the faith, as demonstrated by an entry for William Henry Holroyd for March 1894. He was listed as having being removed from the church records but 'he is not to know of this for his wife's sake'.

One of the most valuable records, and one which most genealogists would love to find in all church records, is the record of events kept by this particular church. The book is a comprehensive diary of happenings at the church on a week to week basis. Events such as visits from other churches, special services and new officials being appointed were all recorded, with plenty of names included. The records also included a diary of services, which recorded what type of service was performed each day, including a summary of the sermon that was preached to the congregation.

Chapter 7

EDUCATION AND INSTITUTIONS

Yorkshire's schools and colleges offered a variety of courses and teaching, some of which was designed to enable people to participate in Yorkshire's various industries. Many of the classes taught, particularly for those who worked in textiles, which required specialist skills and knowledge, were not available anywhere else in the country. The records relating to these courses show just how much commitment was required to complete successfully the programme of study.

Some of our ancestors, despite working long hours, often carrying out hard manual labour, were keen to better themselves and so attended evening classes. This form of education became popular at the end of the nineteenth century and has continued to flourish. Details of the course of study an ancestor followed and programmes from their award ceremonies can give more information about what their education involved.

SCHOOLS

Many people imagine that school records would be an excellent resource for family history research. Whether or not this is true depends upon where your ancestors went to school, whether records for that school have survived and if so what they cover.

Most school records have been deposited with county and local record offices. Some can be extremely useful, with lists of pupils, photographs of school events and even reports on individual scholars. Others are of less interest, comprising simply a school's financial accounts. Some school archives have a thirty-year closure period because of data protection, meaning that more recent records are out of bounds to researchers.

School prospectuses, where they exist, can be useful documents, but it is important to remember that they were written, as prospectuses are now, to impress prospective parents and pupils and so are biased. Nevertheless, they can be useful documents in illustrating how many pupils attended a school, what facilities were on offer and what type of education pupils received.

The following section takes a look at a selection of school records held by North, South, East and West Yorkshire Record Offices. There are thousands of records available, but these examples should show the extent (and the limitations) of what is on offer.

North Yorkshire County Record Office

Records for the Wigglesworth Church of England School date from before the school was even built, starting with the executorship of founder Lawrence Clark's will in 1793, and the subsequent building of the school. The archives include lists of pupils at the school between 1800 and 1865, school administration papers and trustees' minutes.

Sheffield Archives

The records of Penistone Grammar School stretch back some 400 years. This was another school set up via a bequest. The archives contain dozens of items of limited interest, such as accounts books for matters such as the cleaning of the school and building projects. Of more interest to anyone wanting to find out more about an ancestor who attended the school are the photograph collections, which include groups of pupils outside the headmaster's house, dating to the 1890s and aerial and ground shots of the school buildings. There is also a collection of school brochures, printed as guidance to prospective parents, reports by school inspectors and programmes from school concerts in the 1960s.

East Riding of Yorkshire Archives

St Mary's High School in Hull was established in 1905 by the Sisters of Mercy Order. The records that exist for the school date from its foundation to its eventual closure in 1988. Items that would be of interest to anyone whose ancestor attended the school include pupil reports from 1923–9, photographs of pupils and albums of school productions from the 1920s onwards and copies of the school's magazines from the 1930s until the closure of the school.

West Yorkshire Archive Service

The archives of the Leeds Blenheim Middle School cover 100 years of the school's history from the 1870s onwards. There are logbooks and admission registers for girls and boys departments from 1873 and also more recent photographs, film and videos of school activities.

TYPES OF SCHOOL RECORDS

An advert in the *Leeds Mercury* of 27 November 1744, held at Leeds Local Studies Library, is just one of hundreds of adverts that have appeared in newspapers, giving details of teachers required, situations vacant and places at schools. The following advert was for a mistress required at Ledsham Charity School:

> The salary is ten pounds a year, with all accommodation . . . for teaching twenty girls to read, spin & c. the qualifications required are that such mistress be no younger than 25 years, a single woman, has no dependents upon her and be capable of well instructing the children in reading, spinning, sewing & c.

This small advert not only shows what the girls were taught at this school, but underlines the fact that there were obviously no formal qualifications needed for this type of job.

Trade and local directories can give further clues as to what a particular school was like, giving details of whether it was of endowed or charitable status, where it was located, attendance figures and the name of the head-teacher. Forster's Education Act of 1870 allowed for the establishment of a locally elected school board if existing school provision was not adequate. Local newspapers can show that there was often tension around the creation of a school board and whether one should be allowed at all. For example, at Morley near Leeds in 1872, there was an unsuccessful attempt to set up a school board, which caused incessant arguments through the letters page of the local newspaper.

The local history collection at Scarborough public library holds an unnamed Scarborough school logbook for 1880, which gives great detail about the problems faced by the teachers and pupils:

> Jan 5, School reopened in the Unitarian School room as our own room was destroyed by fire during the holidays. All the registers were totally destroyed, together with all the other schools books and a large proportion of the desks and seats. 124 present in the morning.
>
> Jan 9, The single room is too small to give sufficient accommodation for all the scholars.
>
> Jan 16, Numbers much larger this week in fact so large that very little work could be done on account of the room being so crowded.

Although the survival and usefulness of logbooks varies from area to area, they can give valuable information about attendance, the school buildings, the curriculum and even, as we have just seen, the feelings of teachers and the consequences of problems such as the fire discussed by that teacher.

EVENING CLASSES

Most Yorkshire cities, towns and even villages offered a range of evening classes from the mid-nineteenth century onwards. Many were held in local venues such as a church or village hall, others were held in the local school or college.

The records of Bradford's Bolton Usher St college evening classes which cover 1893 to 1901 are held at Bradford archives. The institution was typical of those in a predominantly working-class area; classes were held in the evening so that people could attend after work. The subjects taught were generally of a practical nature, such as sewing or nursing, rather than classes such as art appreciation or creative writing, which would have been held in more affluent areas.

The evening class book is a beautifully handwritten hardback book in which the thoughts and observations of the head of the college Ethel Sharpe are recorded. It is fascinating to read her views on how the classes were progressing and how popular certain subjects were. Ethel even touched on local events through her entries about attendance and the factors which she felt were influencing the number of pupils in each class.

The first was for the academic year 1893–4, at which 366 students were admitted, with almost 100 of the pupils being over 20 years old. The staff who taught the classes for that year were listed as Miss Jackman, Miss Beanland, Miss Wright, Miss Sharpe, Miss Williams and Miss Nicholson. Over the next few months, Ethel noted how many students had attended each week. There are often comments about sickness prevailing in the district, which resulted in a low attendance at the classes. A comment for October 1901 stated that attendance was low because of a 'poor night following wet day, students will not venture out to get wet again'.

That the evening school was subject to government inspection is shown by an entry copied from a government report about the school for 1894:

> Although the numbers of this school show a great falling off during the second half of the session, yet in other respects the teachers are to be congratulated on their successful work.

Entries relating to the cookery classes held often stated which dishes were prepared by the students, showing the type of food which was favoured at that time. It seems to have been plain and wholesome, the menu for September 1895 was lentil soup, bread and butter pudding and rock buns. September 1901 saw the students prepare savoury mince, treacle tart, boiled potatoes and ginger biscuits.

Ethel Sharpe's commentary on the popularity of certain classes and activities is testament to the tastes of the day, which in the case of sewing classes appear to have changed greatly. She wrote that she 'gave a lesson in the cutting out of a flannel petticoat. The girls were much interested and gave pleasing results during the evening.' It is difficult to imagine today's teenage girls showing quite the same enthusiasm!

Student demand led to the introduction of a class in home nursing at Bolton Usher St in 1899 and Nurse Amy Hamilton was enlisted to teach the students. There was also a laundry class, another home-making subject, which seems to have been popular at this time.

Evening classes weren't restricted to schools provided by the government or council. Some commercial bodies and charities also ran day and night classes for members of the public, and their records have often survived.

ADULT EDUCATION IN THE NORTH RIDING

Records held by the North Yorkshire County Record Office give a good indication of the history of adult education from its earliest days during Victorian times. Before this era, it was common for children to leave school at the age of 14 and move straight into an apprenticeship or employment. However, the efforts of early education pioneers such as the Co-operative movement, which we will examine in more detail later in the chapter, meant that adult education classes became more accepted and common. Some employers, such as Titus Salt at Saltaire, offered education classes to adults and provided the facilities for these, believing that those who chose to educate themselves outside working hours would stay away from drink and gambling and be better workers. These philanthropists often had a genuine paternal interest in their workers, and felt that educating those who were willing was another way to be a good employer, providing for all aspects of an employee's well-being.

The first adult education in the Richmond area began as early as 1810, with the establishment of a scientific society, which offered lectures to members. Because of a high subscription charge, membership was mainly confined to the better-off inhabitants of the town. The next step was the foundation of a Mechanics' Institute, in 1825, which was supported by a Lord Dundas of Marske, who was known to be interested in the education of working-class men. There was a subscription fee of 8s a year, which was quite high, as it equated to around a week's wage for a working-class man. Despite the aim of making the institute accessible to all classes, the fact that the rector and various mayors were presidents of the institute during its early years, and also that a separate working men's hall was created in Newbiggin, shows that the institute ended up catering for middle-class people instead.

Congregationalists and other Nonconformist religious groups played a big part in establishing adult education in the county, and the Richmond area was no exception. James Wilkinson, the Congregational minister of Keld, helped to set up workers' institutes at several towns, including Gunnerside, Reeth and Grinton, each of which contained a reading room and a library. Such institutes flourished in Yorkshire Dales towns during the late nineteenth century.

The pattern of lectures for such institutes seems to have been fairly informal, and unstructured, as they did not have the funds to pay for speakers to attend from a long way away, and so local businessmen and dignitaries were often invited to speak about their own special subjects. The libraries at these institutes were very popular, the library at Muker's Improvement Society gathered 300 books in its first year alone and most took books that members donated. Reeth had 850 books in 1878, including Shakespeare plays, some Bronte novels and books on historical and scientific themes. Reeth also had a newsroom, which took several weekly and daily papers.

Most of the Yorkshire Dales institutes had to rely heavily on member contributions and fundraising to continue their existence. Many held annual fundraising concerts, with other lectures in between to raise money.

The Cambridge University Extension Movement was a national attempt to bring learning out of universities and into communities. It reached Richmond in 1884, with a course of twelve lectures, at the end of which seventeen candidates took an examination.

LEEDS UNIVERSITY ARCHIVES

The special collections department at Leeds University library is referred to several times in this book as a useful archive for various family history research topics. The records at the university's Brotherton Library contain archives relating to the history of the university itself and Yorkshire College, the university's forerunner.

The Brotherton Library, in which the special collections department is located, is named after Lord Brotherton (1856–1930), one of the library's main benefactors. Brotherton's collection of books was presented to the library after his death, together with funding to allow the library to grow; there are now over 50,000 books. Brotherton was an important Leeds citizen; he was mayor of the city in 1913–14 and at his own expense raised the 15th Battalion, known as the 'Leeds Pals', who fought in the First World War.

The archives relating to the University of Leeds and to the Yorkshire College would be important to anyone who thinks they may have had an ancestor who taught or learnt at either of these establishments. Metres of shelving at the Brotherton Library are devoted to student records for both the university and the college, dating back to the 1870s. Day, evening and occasional students are all represented on the registers, together with matriculation registers for the Yorkshire College and graduation lists for the university. There are also records of staff who taught at each establishment, and these records include press cuttings about events such as award ceremonies, retirement and obituary notices and the records of various committees attended by students and staff.

THE CO-OPERATIVE MOVEMENT AND EDUCATION

We are familiar with the Co-op stores, which have been on Yorkshire high streets for over 100 years and which are discussed in more detail in Chapter 5. However, as we have seen, the retail and wholesale divisions of the movement were only one aspect of the society's activities. The society was also instrumental in providing early versions of night classes and correspondence courses, activities which were later taken on by public bodies once it was found that there was a demand for lifelong education.

The Co-op's educational activities were formalized in 1882, when the society appointed an education committee. They developed a range of technical correspondence courses and by the beginning of the twentieth century there were over 1,000 students enrolled on courses, which covered subjects including citizenship, history and bookkeeping.

Some of the Co-operative societies had their own reading rooms, bookrooms and libraries, which were open to members. It was enthusiastic use of such facilities by the public which helped to continue the provision of evening classes by local councils and other public bodies. The Co-operative movement set up its own college in 1919, at Holyoake House in Manchester. After the Second World War, the college moved to Stanford Hall near Loughborough and a college still exists today.

CHARITABLE INSTITUTIONS

Charitable institutions were particularly popular during the Victorian era. In an age when many people suffered greatly, there were people who, for moral or religious reasons, wished to help others. Whether your ancestor was a philanthropist, or perhaps called on one of these charities for help, looking for charitable records can give you many clues about them.

Much charity work, particularly during Victorian times, was done by people in positions of power and authority, such as the philanthropist Joseph Rowntree who had a reputation for caring for his workforce. Other relief was provided by churches or organizations set up or funded by religious bodies. Where these records survive, they may relate to those providing the care, or to those who benefited from it. There have been hundreds of different charities. For example, Sheffield archives hold dozens of papers relating to charities in the Doncaster area. These include the Yorkshire Institute for Deaf and Dumb Children, the Home Teaching Association, the Miners' Welfare Club and Institution and the Parish Church Day Schools' Charities.

An eighteenth-century document relating to the care of widows and orphans of Church of England clergy, held at the Borthwick Institute, gives a good example of the type of philanthropy that people of some means could exercise towards those in need of help. The organization was not a charity in the way that we would understand the term today, with anyone being able to contribute as much as they want and whenever they please – people were required to join the organization on an annual or life basis.

The paper is titled 'Rules and orders for the management and disposal of a charitable contribution proposed to be raised for the relief of the widows and orphans and distressed families of the clergy within the deaneries of Doncaster and Pontefract' and dated 21 June 1784. Those who could benefit from the charity, stated the rules, included widows or orphans of clergy who were unprovided for, or sick or ill clergymen. No one was to receive relief without a certificate presenting their case and outlining their need. The paper gave several examples of how a certificate should be set out, giving the name(s) of the applicant(s), their age(s), an assurance that they were unprovided for elsewhere and that they behaved 'decently and soberly and frequents the service of the church of England'.

Financial business was dealt with in the same document, with a payment of ten guineas buying an individual the privilege of life benefactor status and one guinea benefactor status for a year. Among the officers elected for 1795, who are all listed in the document, are a George Pearson of Doncaster (president) and Revd Mr Vollans, rector of Hemsworth (treasurer). Among those subscribing to the charity (again all subscribers are listed by name) were Mrs Fife of Doncaster, Mrs Walker of Middlewood and Mr Martin of Sandal-Parva. Next on the list are those who benefited from the charity, including Elizabeth, daughter of the Revd Thos Pierson, formerly curate of Felkirk, who was awarded £10 and the widow of the Revd Mr Trotter, formerly vicar of Huddersfield, who received a payment of £21. The detail in this document, particularly with regard to names and places, would make identifying a likely ancestor a fairly simple process.

The paper finishes with a look at the charity's finances for the previous financial year. Subscriptions for 1795 were £95 16s 0d, with £1 15s 6d received in interest. The balance for the previous year was £71 7s 11d, with £9 17s 0d arrears, quite a large proportion of the balance of subscriptions.

COUNCIL DOCUMENTS

As we saw in Chapter 4, town and city council papers can be an excellent way of finding out more about how people were treated in their community and what priorities the authorities had at a given time.

The reports for Leeds City Council for 1936/7 include a section on the Blind Persons Act Committee. The city, stated the report, spent £39,000 of rates money on blind people during the financial year 1936/7: the city has 'recognised that the community has an obligation to perform to those unfortunate people who through lack of sight are unable to follow normal vocations'. The paper went on to detail more about what facilities were available for the blind in the city. These included education for blind children at Blenheim Walk school up to the age of 16, after which they were able to follow vocational training at the technical training college for the blind at Barrack Rd. As a result of the training, the committee reported that many blind people were able to work in a trade, some had gone to university and others regularly attended dances, concerts and other social events.

The committee informed the council in their annual report that a district thrift guild had been set up that year, which involved a representative touring houses in the city, asking the public to buy items that had been made in workshops by the blind. Goods for sale included mattresses, knitted items and brushes.

York City Archives.

CASE STUDY: YORK CITY ARCHIVES WORKHOUSE RECORDS

The collection of workhouse records held at York city archives are an excellent example of variety of documents that can be used in this area of family history research. Although people are mentioned by name in many of the records we will explore, some of the later correspondence files, from the second half of the twentieth century onwards, are not open to the public, because of data protection. Nevertheless, there are still plenty of documents available that can show what life was like in a workhouse, what it was like to be an inmate or a member of staff and to what degree the outside world was involved with workhouse communities.

The correspondence papers concern staff wages, sickness, conditions of service and applications for staff vacancies. These give an idea of the type of work undertaken by staff members of a workhouse and what sort of conditions they would have worked under. Records for the city's Grange workhouse include a list of vagrants covering 1848–67 and a list of ex-servicemen residing at the Grange. The list stated whether or not each man was bedridden and whether the person smoked cigarettes or a pipe (all of them smoked!). Another list featuring names is for boys and girls who were put into farm service between 1910 and 1914 and a further useful list of names is the register of births in the workhouse between 1886 and 1945.

The paupers' case papers for various workhouses in the York district cover all aspects of workhouse life, from celebrations to misbehaviour, with the added bonus of featuring the names of many individuals. Among the papers are warrants for the arrest of an individual absconding with workhouse clothing in 1906, warrants dealing with the wilful neglect of children by individuals and information about those who refused to carry out assigned tasks in the workhouse wards.

However, not all the papers are concerned with gloomy aspects of workhouse life. There is information about the parties that were planned for various events such as armistice celebrations and visiting arrangements for friends and family of workhouse inmates. One case related is that of a workhouse cook who got herself into trouble with her bosses for feeding her husband when he visited her workplace kitchens during his lunch break. Another concerned a relative asking for one of the inmates to visit his home for a week. However, he specified that the inmate must bring along his ration book, as he hadn't brought it on his previous visit and the family had struggled to feed him.

Dozens of the workhouse records held at this archive are related to the day-to-day running of the various institutions. Although they are sparse on actual names they are a good record of what exactly was needed to keep a workhouse running and the kind of preparation that went on behind the scenes. Useful items include a 1918 account of workhouse food stocks, account books including entries for matrons' clothing, firewood, funerals, garden materials and pigs. Inmates' property registers give an idea of the kind of possessions people brought into the workhouse and inventory books can include items such as artificial limbs, optical and dental requirements; various goods needed for people of all ages.

Nowadays, we are used to a welfare state which helps to care for those who are not able to contribute to society by earning a living. But in earlier times disabled or ill people often had the workhouse as their only option. Registers held at York City archives, such as the register of persons of unsound mind for 1936–50 or the patients detained under the Lunacy Act of 1890 for 1948–53 illustrate the plight of those who had no friends or family to care for them and were forced to seek refuge in the workhouse.

Chapter 8

UNIFORMED ANCESTORS

Many of our ancestors lived through times of war and conflict and some of them would have been in active service. Not only is it possible to find out more about an ancestor who was part of the armed forces or who fought in wartime, there are several Yorkshire archives that can help with research into what it was like to take part in a war. Other records can be useful for researching those ancestors who were part of the uniformed services.

ARMY RECORDS

Tracing an ancestor who served in the military through army records is a specialized area of genealogy, and a good proportion of the records required are based at the National Archives in London. These include records of individual soldiers, medal rolls and details of officers' commissions.

There have been regiments in England since the 1750s, and each regiment had its own number, with a regiment being the basic British army unit. From 1881, many regiments were merged and it was at this time that regiments began to be linked to a specific county, for example, the North, South, East and West Yorkshire regiments, all active after 1881 in the Cardwell reforms.

In order to trace the service record of an ancestor as a British officer, you need to know their regiment. Service records for 1920 onwards are not yet available to the public and are kept by the Ministry of Defence, being available only to the next of kin, upon payment of a fee. Pre-1920 records are mostly kept at the National Archives, and further details are in the 'military history' section of their website (www.nationalarchives.gov.uk).

If all this sounds like Yorkshire army ancestors are out of reach, don't despair. There are still plenty of ways to find out about those who either served in a war or who lived through the hostilities as a member of the public.

Many of our ancestors would have lived through a war at some point in their lives, but it was the First and Second World Wars that had most impact on the general public. Unlike previous wars, these two conflicts involved large sections of communities being enlisted into military service and the majority of remaining adults engaged in the war effort in other ways. This chapter will explain how to find out more about what it was like to live through a war and how background research can reveal more about our twentieth-century wartime ancestors.

LOCAL NEWSPAPERS

Local newspapers can be invaluable for finding out what life was like for people during wartime. Although it was not always possible for the press to print exactly what was happening to troops and where battles were being fought or which towns had been raided and how the war was going, they are an excellent barometer of public feeling. Local newspapers described events that were going on both locally and nationally, as well as giving information about local heroes and those who lost their lives to the war.

The *Yorkshire Post* for 1 January 1941 carried an article about the problem of recruiting firewatchers. There weren't enough firewatchers to cover the number of businesses that had to be protected. Every firm which employed more than 30 people or had a bigger capacity than 50,000 cubic feet was required to have firewatchers. The same issue of the paper also carried a table of times for the blackouts, which ran from around 5.30 p.m. to 8.45 a.m. On the same theme, British Railways had placed a large advert in the newspaper, about overcrowding on trains caused by blackouts. The advert pleaded with people to try to finish work a little earlier and so ease the strain on the already overcrowded rush hour trains. Millions of people were leaving work in time to be home before the blackout, meaning that there weren't enough spaces on the train for everyone.

Still on the wartime theme, a Dr George Cockroft, medical officer to the Leyburn Rural District Council, was reported by the *Yorkshire Post* to have recommended that the public consume only one course of food at each mealtime, to reduce pressure on food supplies caused by rationing and the difficulty of obtaining foodstuffs from overseas during times of conflict. The article went on to give a suggested menu, which provides an interesting insight into the sort of food that would have been eaten during the war years. Dr Cockroft suggested a kipper, brown bread and a cup of coffee for breakfast, a lunch of a rissole and bread, teatime would be an 'ordinary plain tea', followed by a supper of a sausage and oatcakes.

Finding food supplies was obviously a big problem as the newspaper also carried a piece on butchers in Otley, West Yorkshire, who had decided that, because of the problem of obtaining meat supplies, they would open their shops each week only from Thursday onwards.

As well as the terrible losses suffered by Yorkshire communities during times of war, civilians had to face danger in their own towns and cities, when disasters happened as part of everyday life. The Low Moor explosion of 1916 in Bradford resulted in 39 deaths but was hardly reported in local newspapers, as the Ministry of Munitions felt that the accident was sensitive information that couldn't be relayed in full, because of the fear of giving information to the enemy.

Word of mouth proved stronger than newspaper reporting after the accident, and a rumour went round that workers had fled from the chemical explosion with their skin dyed yellow from the picric acid they had been working with. There had been a tremendous explosion and houses in the streets around were damaged by flying debris from the blast. The *Bradford Daily Telegraph* reported only that a Yorkshire munitions factory had suffered an explosion and that there had been 20 fatalities. This is a reminder that, although local newspapers can be a good source of information about what was happening during wartime, they were not always able to report fully on certain events.

THE HOME FRONT

Most of us are aware of the debt we owe to the thousands of people who were actively involved in fighting for the country over the past few centuries. But, particularly, during the First and Second World Wars, there were countless people who remained at home, but who were contributing to the war effort.

Information held by the Wakefield headquarters of West Yorkshire archives gives a flavour of what the researcher can expect to find on the home front. For the Second World War, there is a collection of papers relating to the aftermath and consequences of air raids in the local area. These include lists of properties damaged in air raids. One such report for 14 March 1941 for Wakefield described how two bombs fell, damaging property extensively and trapping and injuring the unfortunate occupants. The report went on to name the people killed or injured, house by house, and described the rescues.

The Wakefield City Fire Brigade also made reports to their district officer on fires caused by bombs at various times during the Second World War. A report for 16/17 September 1940 described the private housing that had been hit as well as damage to the prison yard and railway station. There are lists of the names and addresses of air raid wardens and first aid officers. A school logbook for the war years gave fascinating detail of what life was like during the bombing raids. It described how attendance was often poor the day after a bombing raid and how classrooms could be damaged during the raids, causing problems in teaching the children in the following weeks because the rooms were ruined by the fallout from the bombs.

A loose-leaf proclamation dating from May 1917 forms part of the records of the Catholic Apostolic Church in Horton, Bradford, now at the Borthwick

Wakefield Town Hall.

Institute, York, and shows how methods of communication have changed since the First World War. The proclamation was to be read at all UK churches and chapels for four consecutive weeks. Reading the document out to religious congregations was obviously one of the most effective means of transmitting information to a large group of people during that period, something which is almost inconceivable nowadays.

The address, which was from King George V, urged his fellow countrymen to abstain from 'all unnecessary consumption of grain'. The king advised all heads of house to reduce household consumption of bread by at least a quarter, not to allow flour to be used in pastry-making and not to bake any other goods except bread. Only those holding a special licence were to give grain or oats to horses, in the hope that unnecessary consumption of grain would conserve food supplies, helping to bring the war 'to a speedy end'.

WAR MEMORIALS

The county of Yorkshire has numerous war memorials dedicated mainly to those who gave their lives in the First and Second World Wars. They are sited in countless locations, from sleepy villages to busy city centres. Most list those who were living in that particular town or village before they fought for their country.

The Bradford war memorial was unveiled on 1 July 1922, on the sixth

Yorkshire's war memorials remember those who gave their lives for their country.

anniversary of the Battle of the Somme. This was a particular poignant anniversary to Bradfordians, as that battle had caused terrible losses to the Bradford Pals regiment. The toll the First World War had taken on the city was shown by the fact that there were 37,000 names on the roll of honour, and only 3,000 more people than this attended the unveiling of the monument.

The Bradford Pals were just two battalions of thousands who eagerly signed to serve their country at the outbreak of the First World War. Pals battalions were made up of friends and workmates who lived in the same area and would serve their country alongside each other. Tragically, when the losses were heavy, such as on 1 July 1916 on the Somme, the community where the soldiers came from would be shattered. In the first hour of the battle alone, 1,700 men had been killed or injured and the loss was heavier by the end of the battle. Bradford newspapers during the days after the battle, which is still the day of heaviest losses in the history of the British Army, tell of the community's horror as it became apparent how many deaths had occurred. Passport style photographs of the soldiers who had perished were shown alongside descriptions of the careers of those men.

THE LIDDLE COLLECTION

The Liddle Collection, based at the special collections department of the University of Leeds library is a set of archives which can help anyone interested in finding out more about what it was like to take part in, or live through, the two world wars. As the papers in the Liddle Collection are arranged alphabetically, there is also the possibility of finding an ancestor named in the archives.

The Liddle Collection was established over 30 years ago to preserve first-hand accounts of what it was like to fight in the First and Second World Wars. The archive includes letters, diaries, personal papers and photographs. The collection contains 30 sections, arranged according to the type of war service and geographical location. There are papers for around 4,000 First World War and 500 Second World War men and women. A catalogue describes all the individual papers, which are mostly filed alphabetically by name within each section. For example, the collection for Italy comprises nine boxes of personal papers of men who fought on the Italian front in the First World War. The papers are filed by surname and there are also maps, photographs and recollections, which form part of a subgroup to the papers of named individuals. Another section is titled 'women' and consists of 182 boxes relating to women who served overseas during the First World War, mainly in nursing. The records include memories of those who served with the Women's Royal Air Force, War Hospitals and the Women's Royal Naval Service. A conscientious objectors collection provides a different viewpoint to military service, as does a collection relating to life on the domestic front.

THE SECOND WORLD WAR EXPERIENCE CENTRE

The Second World War Experience Centre, based in Horsforth, Leeds, was established in 1998 to preserve a huge variety of sources relating to the Second World War. Since opening, the centre has established a name as a respected place to research books, TV programmes and family history.

Since 2003, the centre has been a registered museum and not only keeps relevant material, but actively restores and preserves items. The centre's aim is to encourage the public to access its records – great news for family historians. Even better is their ethos of collecting not only material relating to Second World War service people, but to everyone whose lives were touched by the war, including civilians, prisoners and conscientious objectors.

The centre's collections are grouped under five main sections; war at sea, war in the air, war on land, civilians' war and clandestine war. The latter covers elite special forces for both allied and enemy forces. Perhaps the most valuable material to anyone hoping find out more about what it was like to have lived through, or fought in the Second World War, are the diaries,

The Second World War Experience Centre, Horsforth.

personal letters and tape recordings which have been donated to the archive by members of the public.

Also useful are the various records of veterans' associations which have also made the archive their home. One of the archive's latest acquisitions is material relating to the work of women in the Auxiliary Air Force. The centre's website (www.war-experience.org) has testimonies from some of those who signed up to the service, giving their memories of everything from chemical warfare training to their opinion of standard issue underwear.

The Second World War Experience Centre have catalogued their material very comprehensively on the Access to Archives website (www.a2a.org.uk). Here, after selecting the centre in the 'location of archives' menu, you are able to browse all the centre's holdings in detail. They have a large collection of taped material, concerning the experiences of those who lived through the Second World War, whether in active service or on the home front.

One of the booklets held by the centre is *What We Did in the War*, a publication produced in support of the Keighley Senior Health Awareness Project based in West Yorkshire, which contains reminiscences of dozens of Keighley women who contributed to the war effort. Their experiences cover work in munitions factories, mills, hospitals and helping out with evacuees. The topics they talk about in the booklet would have been typical of those of hundreds of women in the Yorkshire area during the Second World War.

Joyce Molloy talked about her work in a munitions factory making shells for spitfires. She recalled that the radio was constantly playing during their 14-hour shifts. The day shift would finish at 7.30 p.m., after which the workers would walk home three or more miles.

Mary Preston had friends who worked in the Women's Land Army and remembered hearing about how bad the food was for the women recruits. She said that friends told her the prisoners of war received much better rations and would urge the women to throw away their own food and share with them instead.

The Sir Montague Burton letters are one of the most interesting collections of correspondence held by the centre. Burton was the founder of the Burton's tailoring empire, still active on today's high streets. He was a Russian Jewish immigrant who began his tailoring business in Leeds and employed thousands of Yorkshire people in his clothing factories. The letters in the collection were written by Burton between 1943 and 1945 to his son Raymond who was serving in the Royal Artillery in Ceylon and India. They are typewritten in diary form and give an insight into the life of one of Yorkshire's most important businessmen during the war years.

As a member of several important societies, including the Ministry of Information, Burton was at the forefront of the 'home front' war effort. For instance, in 1943, the sub-basement of his factory was requisitioned by the ministry of supply for use in refurbishing and reissuing clothing and uniforms. Burton also commented on his opinion of the progress of the war, informing his son as early as September 1944 that textile production was switching from the production of military uniforms to demob suits, in readiness for victory in the war.

Burton attended many major social events in and around the Leeds area during the war and his letters to his son described the functions and named others who attended. He visited a YMCA shelter in the city, to see first hand the work done there in providing bed and board at short notice for military and civilians alike.

The last few letters in the collection concerned Burton's preparing himself and his family for peacetime. In May 1945 he advised Raymond that he and his two brothers had been made into directors of the Burtons' firm, saying of the end of the war; 'there is a sigh of relief everywhere that the nightmare is almost over'. He advised his son that he and his wife would suspend their celebrations for the end of the war until the whole family were back safely together, a sentiment which must surely have been echoed by countless other families at that time.

YORKSHIRE AIR MUSEUM

The museum, based near York has an archive, library and research centre which is open to researchers by appointment. The archive contains an extensive aviation library, as well as documents and photographs about RAF, RAAF and RCAF squadrons that served in the county. Although staff are happy to help with initial enquiries, researchers are asked for a donation to go towards the cost of collecting and maintaining the archive, for any research they do.

The rest of the museum contains a collection of 40 international aircraft, in the historic setting of a former airfield. Visitors are able to take a virtual tour of a Halifax bomber and see some of the uniforms worn by Yorkshire air crews during the Second World War. The museum is also home to what is believed to be the only air-gunners' collection in the world. The collection is dedicated to the 20,000 air gunners who lost their lives in the Second World War, at a time when most could only expect to live two weeks after beginning the job. The display shows the weapons the air gunners worked with and explains the techniques they used in aerial combat.

This archive holds numerous files pertaining to mainly bomber squadrons based in Yorkshire and Lincolnshire during the Second World War. These files are in three sections containing squadron history, memorabilia and photographs, most of which have been donated by ex-squadron members and enthusiasts. The archive also holds miscellaneous sections of RAF Forms 540 and 541 Squadron Operational Records. The museum's library contains around 13,000 books on aviation subjects and the files contain such diverse subjects as registers of private pilot's licence holders, who was who in aviation, RFG training in the First World War, the Air Transport Auxiliary, plus information on aviation celebrities.

LAW AND ORDER

Many of us think that our ancestors would have been law-abiding people, who wouldn't have had any brushes with the law. In fact, it was probably easier to fall foul of the law during previous centuries than it is today. Bankruptcy and poverty could place someone at odds with the authorities, because some people found it necessary to steal in order to survive.

Regardless of the rights and wrongs of this, if your ancestor did have dealings with the police or courts, you might actually find more out about them than you would a law-abiding ancestor who never came to the attention of the authorities. As in so many areas of family history research, it is the out of the ordinary which has often survived and in this section, we will look at what records exist in Yorkshire relating to law and order and how these could relate to our own ancestors.

The justice system which governed the population of England until the 1970s was established in the 1361 Statute of Westminster at which justices of the peace were established to hear court cases in each county. These justices met four times a year at what were called quarter sessions. Quarter sessions papers are a commonly referred to source in family history and can provide plenty of useful information about law and order, as well as about particular individuals. By the eighteenth century, the justices were not only responsible for law and order, but also the administration of the poor law, regulations of prices and the upkeep of bridges and highways. The quarter session system was finally abolished in 1971.

The North Riding Court of quarter sessions records are held at North Yorkshire County Record Office, West Riding records are held at Wakefield archives and records for the East Riding at the East Ridings of Yorkshire Archives Service. Some boroughs had their own quarter sessions and their records are usually at the town's archives, rather than the county offices.

Among the business dealt with at quarter sessions were coroners' inquests. Coroners, who investigated sudden or suspicious deaths, had to claim back their expenses by sending in inquest returns. These noted only the name of the deceased, the date of the inquest and the verdict of the jury. Local newspapers, however, particularly in the case of a sensational or notorious death, may have many more details in their news pages around the date of an inquest.

A useful source of the names of ancestors are indictment books, which recorded all serious criminal charges that were brought before county magistrates in quarter sessions from the mid-seventeenth century onwards. For each case, indictment books contained the name, address and occupation of the defendant, details of the offence, what plea was made, the jury's decision and details of the sentence handed down.

The Wakefield office of the West Yorkshire Archive Service holds material relating to the West Yorkshire police force. Among the most useful documents to historians tracing a family member who was in the force are examination books. These can be used to chart the career of an individual and include details of any medals or awards won.

North Yorkshire County Record Office holds records relating to the North Riding police force. Among the holdings are a police charge book for 1854–6, including photographs of those appearing at quarter sessions, and a police pensions register for 1865–1927. Access to the North Riding police force records is currently under review by the police authority, so anyone wishing to consult the documents would have to contact the North Yorkshire County Record Office in advance to check the current position.

Many of the records for the police forces who covered South Yorkshire are held at Sheffield archives. Again, the archives are not freely available and staff at the archives can advise how permission to view the archives should be sought. Archives for the Hull City Police, East Riding Constabulary and North-East Yorkshire police are held at the East Riding of Yorkshire Archives Service at Beverley.

The police service often used local newspapers as a way of passing on good news from within the force, for example, publicizing award ceremonies or occasions when a member of a force had been decorated for bravery. A July 1968 edition of the *Telegraph and Argus* newspaper mentioned four police officers who had been given medals by the Chief Constable of the West Riding Sir George Scott. Constable Frank Gordon Rose of Skipton, Chief Inspector Robert Oates of Dewsbury and Constable John Swires Escott of Shipley all received medals for long service and good conduct. Constable Richard Bond of Heckmondwike was awarded a certificate of merit by the Royal Society of Prevention of Cruelty to Animals after rescuing a dog from a beck.

This type of publicity was of interest to the newspaper's readers and had the added benefit of publicizing the work of the police force to the general public.

Chapter 9

MIGRATION AND POVERTY

For centuries Yorkshire had a reputation as being a place of plentiful employment. People travelled to the region from all over the world but sometimes entered a labour market that was already saturated. Racial hatred and poor living conditions were often the lot of immigrants. Large cities such as Sheffield and Leeds had whole areas populated by people from a particular country. Census returns and trade directories can help to give an idea of the ethnic makeup of a particular district.

IMMIGRATION

For centuries, England has been the destination of people migrating from all over the world, partly because of its industrial heritage, which has provided millions of jobs. There have been several waves of immigration, usually triggered by events abroad. However, until the last century, there was little attempt to record arrivals or departures from the country and so records can be sketchy.

The first large waves of immigrants arrived from Europe, particularly France and the Low Countries during the sixteenth century. These people tended to stay around London, where they were able to find work easily. It wasn't until the nineteenth century, when Yorkshire became such a strong player in the Industrial Revolution, that immigrants reached the county in any numbers.

The potato famine that began in Ireland in 1845 and the pogroms of the Russian Empire were just some of the big events that caused people to leave their homelands to begin a new life in England, moving to Yorkshire for work. The twentieth century saw several further waves of immigration, triggered mainly by the two world wars, bringing refugees from Eastern Europe. These were followed by immigrants from Commonwealth countries, eager to make the most of the freedom of colonists to come and go as they wished. Many of those who arrived from Pakistan, India and Jamaica took jobs in textile mills, particularly in West Yorkshire.

Many native English people had left their jobs in textiles during the Second World War and were unwilling to return to what some felt was poorly paid work in bad working conditions. This gap in the labour market was filled by immigrants, who would send money home to their families rather than uprooting their wives and children, at least until they'd made a stable life for themselves.

Many immigrants would find their way to the county by word of mouth, hearing that jobs were available in the county's mills, mines and on farmland. They would also tend to move to areas where people of their own nationality had already settled. Although this gave them the advantage of living in a familiar community, there was a danger of ghettos developing and native people turning against immigrants.

TRACING IMMIGRANT ANCESTORS

Census records

Census returns can be an excellent way to find out not only when immigrant ancestors arrived in an area, but also to examine the ethnic makeup of an area. The first English census which is any use for family history research purposes is the 1841 census, but it is only from the 1851 census onwards that enumerators recorded where a person had been born; the 1841 census only records if someone originated from 'foreign parts'.

When you have found your individual or family on the census, take a look at the returns for the houses and streets around the home of your ancestors. This way, you will be able to identify what proportion of their neighbours came from the same country, what sort of occupation the majority of the neighbourhood followed (for example, professional or manual), and the number of people who lived in each house. Many immigrant communities were notorious for overcrowding, with foreigners being forced, through lack of money or little local knowledge, to take the poorest accommodation on offer, in the worst areas.

Alien records

The Aliens Act of 1905 followed a Royal Commission report after the 1901 census that revealed almost 300,000 'aliens' (foreign people) made up part of the country's population of almost 41.5 million. The commission concluded that aliens were causing crime, anarchy and spreading disease.

The Act required all aliens of adult age (16 and above) to register with the police. Not all of these registers have survived, but they do exist in several Yorkshire local record offices. The Wakefield archives hold a record of aliens for 1948–65 as part of the records of the West Riding Constabulary.

Doncaster archives hold papers relating to a Jan Curkanow of Warsaw. They show what type of paperwork was required for someone to move from one country to another. The records include a certificate of identity issued to Curkanow, who was born in 1913, by the office of the military governor of the USA zone of Germany in 1948. The archives also have a certificate which was issued under the Alien's Order of 1920, which Curkanow held whilst she lived in Doncaster.

Oral history

The local studies library at Bradford Central library holds an extensive oral history collection covering immigration. The recordings were made by the Bradford Heritage Recording Unit in the 1980s and appear in the library in transcribed book form. Each interview is contained within a separate book and there is a summary folder of each interview, outlining the main subjects covered during the conversation.

The topics covered include the feelings of the interviewee about making a new life in Yorkshire, attitudes towards culture clashes and racism, arranged marriages and the difficulties of settling in a foreign country. Each interview obviously only features one person's opinion, but they are a helpful way to find out what problems affected immigrants when they arrived in Yorkshire, the issues that were important to them and their feelings about the environment around them.

The transcriptions do not quote actual names, simply the person's sex, age and the date that they arrived in Yorkshire. They cover many different ages and nationalities and, in so doing, demonstrate various viewpoints. One of the interviews relates to a female Asian woman, born in 1957, who moved to the UK when she was 12 years old. Her attitudes towards her life in England are very positive. She told the interviewer that she had always encouraged her children to learn both Punjabi and English, in the hope that they would be able to secure work with their bilingual skills. She also, against opposition from her traditional husband, gained office work after attending night school to learn typing, shorthand and how to translate Punjabi to English and vice versa. Her determination to better herself shines through the transcription.

Another interview is not as positive, but gives a view of the less rosy side of moving to a new country. The male interviewed was a Muslim who was born in the early 1930s and came to Yorkshire in the 1960s. He experienced racism first hand whilst working as a bus driver and also found hostility after an outbreak of smallpox in Bradford in the 1960s, when a Pakistani male was accused of bringing the disease to the UK. Although the interviewee felt proud of his Pakistani culture and wished to uphold it wherever he could, he felt certain that he would let his children arrange their own marriages – an example of how strongly held ideals can change in a different environment.

MIGRATION

Among the groups of ancestors most difficult to trace must be those who had no fixed address, such as the Romany people. As we discovered in Chapter 5, which covered the National Fairground Archive, travelling folk often evaded official record keeping. The Romany Collection, based at Leeds University, is one of the UK's principal collections of books and records relating to Romany culture.

The Romany Collection

The Romany Collection contains over 1,000 items, including many rare objects relating to gypsy culture and particularly the Romany way of life. The collection includes biographies of gypsies and books and pamphlets about Romany customs, such as birth, marriage and funeral rites. There are also playbills from Romany shows and accounts of big events such as annual horse fairs and clan gatherings. Music, letters and photographs build up a more in-depth picture of what life on the road would have been like for a gypsy ancestor.

The Romany Collection was donated to Leeds Library by Dorothy Una Ratcliffe in 1950. It is very much a growing archive, with material being donated from various sources at regular intervals. Those tracing an ancestor who they know or suspect to have been a travelling person may be in for some difficulties, as these groups of people were traditionally able to avoid officialdom. But a visit to the Romany Collection is one way to find out more about what life was like in a caravan, living separately to the rest of society.

The books and pamphlets that make up a good proportion of the collection are written both about and by gypsies. One fascinating pamphlet is *Gypsy Funeral Customs* by Stewart Sanderson. This describes the rituals surrounding gypsy funerals of the last century. Customs observed included the destruction by fire of a gypsy caravan once its occupant had passed away. Sanderson wrote about learning of a gypsy funeral in Romney during the early 1900s, where the corpse was laid out in a tent the night before the funeral. The tent was lit by candles and the Romany men took it in turns to sit with the corpse throughout the night, making sure that no one person was ever left alone with the body. The following morning, gypsy friends and relatives from far and wide arrived to attend the funeral ceremony. Many were dressed in red, the traditional colour of mourning for gypsies, and even horses were plumed with red rosettes. Each person processed past the open coffin and placed a gift, such as a coin or charm, inside. The caravan's possessions were given to the dead man's wife and the caravan then burnt to the ground.

Another valuable text is *Yorkshire Gypsy Fairs, Customs and Caravans* by E Alan Jones (Hutton Press, 1986). The book details how Yorkshire came to be a place of secure living for families, as well as hosting several of the most important fairs in the country. The book states that, in the mid-nineteenth century, employment was extremely high.

> The demand for horses to pull delivery vehicles was great. Who better to supply these needs than the gypsy people? . . . Working from the countryside . . . and from the cities where there was a demand for labour, the traveller could manage a living.

The book also goes into details about other traditional trades carried out by travelling people including tin smithing, basket making, collecting scrap metal, casual farm labour and buying and selling. The basket making was something that could involve the whole family, with quite young children fetching and carrying the raw materials and learning how to make the baskets.

Much of the work described was casual labour that could be abandoned if the family wished, or were forced to move on by hostile people around them. Jones points out that not all communities welcomed gypsy families into their midst, and there was often prejudice and fears about robberies. He says that it is easy to feel that life in a horse-drawn gypsy caravan was an idyllic one, with families travelling picturesque roads, without a care in the world. But he asks the reader to imagine waking in an unheated caravan on a frosty morning, everything you touched freezing cold. You would have had to break a bowl of ice before you could wash or even have a cup of tea.

St Nicholas Church in North Newbald, East Riding of Yorkshire, is particularly associated with gypsy communities, with many Yorkshire families still using the church as a base for family events such as funerals and christenings. Some Romany families moved from fair to fair all summer, meeting friends and relatives on an annual basis. Many of the fairs had medieval roots and had been set up by Royal Charter. Among the most popular fairs were Lee Gap, Seamer, Topcliffe and Brough Hill. Most of these were popular trading places for horses, with details sealed traditionally with a handshake.

Gypsy Lifestyles by John McLaughlin (Lexington books, 1980) looks at the different gypsy communities that have existed, using various generalizations to show the lifestyles. For example, he stated that older members of a gypsy community would have had the most respect from the others in the clan, but that males were always given precedence over females. McLaughlin wrote that females were expected to serve the meal to the men of the house, but not sit at the table themselves. They would eat what they could whilst the men of the family were dining at the table. The more children a gypsy woman had, the higher her status was within the group. McLaughlin also states that most gypsy communities lived by a code of strict moral standards but did not necessarily care for the laws of the country they lived in.

'Mahrime' was a state of defilement or pollution that could come about in various ways. A woman could be considered mahrime after giving birth, until six months had passed. She would be excluded from all social functions, even the christening of her newborn child. A crime could also cause someone to be considered defiled and they would stay in the state of mahrime until the matter had been brought before the 'Kris', a type of gypsy court. McLaughlin describes the court as being subject to the moral approval of those in the community around it. Both parties in a case would swear to abide by its decision and, in taking this public vow, would be held to their promise by peer pressure.

A Romany wedding is different to church or civil ceremonies in the wider world. There was a wedding feast, the sharing of bread, salt and wine, a benediction recited by one of the tribe elders and a headscarf placed on the bride's head. 'Zeita' is the ceremony of bringing the new bride to her home and here there would be a mock struggle between the families of the bride and groom. The bride would spend her first night in the same room as her mother in law.

One of the proudest claims that a Romany person could make was that they were 'born on the straw'. To prepare for a birth, a Romany woman would put straw under the family's caravan and this is where she would give birth to her child. It was also a Yorkshire tradition for a newborn Romany baby to be washed in a stream as soon as possible after the birth.

Some of the books in the Romany Collection are biographies, which give first hand accounts of what the life was like. *The Book of Boswell* is the autobiography of Silvester Gordon Boswell (Victor Gollancz, 1970) and tells the life of Boswell, who was born in Blackpool, Lancashire, in 1895. Boswell described his childhood as a free and happy time when his mother worked in the seaside resort of Blackpool as a palmist.

> We could play in the sand all day round our home and bathe in the sea when we liked all the summer through, when thousands of other children would only get the privilege once a year.

The book includes photographs of Boswell's family members and also of wider groups of friends that he encountered through his life. His own father and grandfather had earned their livings in the boxing booths, fighting for money with anyone who would challenge them and place a bet.

Boswell himself left school at the age of 12 and joined a group of boys, making his living poaching, doing odd jobs and taking whatever work he could find. Before he left, he remembers his mother and father taking over and running the gypsy mission tent. This was a travelling building that would preach to the local gypsy population. Both his parents were gypsy preachers and led the worship and hymn singing. Boswell remembers that they were paid by a monthly cheque and that contributions from worshippers kept the tent in good repair.

POVERTY

It was not just people arriving from overseas that were migrants. Often poor people, on the fringes of society, were forced to move from town to town, avoiding the authorities and seeking charity where they could.

Before 1834, individual Yorkshire areas had responsibility for law and order within their boundaries. Officials had to oversee matters such as building roads, administering charitable benefits and caring for the sick, poor and aged. Yorkshire is different to the rest of the country because the unit of local government was a township, rather than the parish, as was the case in most of the rest of England.

In the rest of England, the parish chest, containing important documents such as bastardy bonds and settlement certificates, has been traditionally kept with parish registers. Both the registers and the chest have then been transferred to a local register office at some time. But because Yorkshire was governed through townships rather than parishes, parish chests were often non-existent and so the documents that would have been kept there have not survived as well as for the rest of the country.

This does not mean, however, that there are not any valuable records to draw on about the poor of a community. One of the finest collections in the county is held at the North Yorkshire County Record Office and contains over 3,000 items relating to those who oversaw parish relief between 1699 and 1927.

The job of parish overseer began in the reign of Queen Elizabeth I and was a varied position, involving the following:

* Raising from parish members stocks of material, such as thread and iron, to be used to make work for the poor.

* Finding work or apprenticeships for children whose parents couldn't support them.

* Finding work for anyone with no trade and no means of supporting themselves independently.

* Raising money for those unable to work, including the ill and handicapped.

The reason so many poor people moved from place to place is that, following the Poor Law Act of 1601, each parish was responsible for providing for the poor within its boundaries. A parish was unwilling to pay for anyone who had not been born within its borders. The settlement certificates issued as a result of these ruings are a way of tracing those ancestors who had fallen on hard times.

Settlement certificates

Some of the settlement certificates held by the North Yorkshire County Record Office relate to the township of Guisborough. A settlement certificate was a document issued to a person who wished to leave a parish by the churchwardens and overseers of the poor for that parish. The document guaranteed to any new parish where that person might settle that, should the person in the future come to be in need of relief, the original parish would provide for them and any dependants.

The new parish would keep the certificate as an insurance against any future claim for relief. Anyone who was not entitled to relief was swiftly dispatched to another parish, as the following examples from the Guisborough collection show:

A boy of 10 years old, with no named father, was ordered to be removed to Stockton in 1800. Hannah O'Neill and her two-week-old child were sent from Guisborough to Stockton in 1817, when they were found not to be legally settled, and Mary Earl, a widow, was refused relief in Slingsby in 1840, when the overseers decided she was not entitled to help.

Relief of children

Another important duty of a parish overseer was to ensure that any children who were dependent on parish relief were found work as quickly as possible. This meant that they would not be a drain on parish resources. The earliest records concerning such duties in the North Yorkshire County Record Office date to 1718, and involve a John Reed, who was put to be a tailor's apprentice. The rules given on how the child should conduct himself give an interesting indication of the possible dangers and temptations the parish officials anticipated:

> . . . fornication or adultery he shall not commit, taverns or alehouses
> he shall not haunt or frequent unless it be about his master's business,
> at dice, cards, tables, bowls or any other unlawful games he shall
> not play.

Letters

Not as formal, but no less illuminating for family historians, are letters written to the overseers of a parish asking for relief. Many of these have a response handwritten on the letter itself, indicating whether or not the plea was answered.

There are over 300 letters held at North Yorkshire Record Office concerning those begging for help. These give much useful information about wages and working conditions, as well as about the individual circumstances of those throwing themselves on the mercy of the parish.

For example, a Robert Williamson was employed at Boulby Alum Works in 1799, but wrote to the overseers that he suffered from fits and so was unable to work with any regularity, having to rely on catching moles for his main means of supporting himself.

In another letter, William Fenton asked the Guisborough overseers to help his wife and five children while he undertook a sail to Botany Bay in 1803. He called upon their aid in a very appealing manner: 'Necessity compels me to solicit that philanthropy which has ever characterised the officers of Guisborough . . . ' Margaret Dale of Sunderland wrote to the Guisborough officers that the river was frozen and she could find no work, and so required assistance from the parish. 'No answer to be made' is the comment written on her letter by a parish official.

Minute books

Like the above letters, parish minute books are a good resource for anyone whose ancestors may have relied on parish relief during their lives. These books, which for most areas of Yorkshire relate to the nineteenth century, give details of meetings where parish officers decided how to treat those who had come to them for help.

The business covered in these meetings could range from small matters, such as a parishioner requesting a warm winter coat, or a few shillings towards their rent, to more formal matters such as the appointment of a governor for the township's poor house.

The Poor Law Amendment Act of 1834 replaced the obligation of individual parishes to care for their own poor with groups, or unions, of parishes who provided relief only through the workhouse. The three ridings of Yorkshire had between them hundreds of workhouses, in both urban and rural locations.

The workhouse

Novels by writers such as Charles Dickens have given the public an idea of how terrible life could be in a workhouse, and how such a place was dreaded by people from all sections of society. Most of us would hate to think that any of our ancestors had been in a workhouse, but many people, because of illness, unemployment or a death in the family, were forced to take the last resort and admit themselves to their local workhouse.

Workhouses were first brought into widespread use with the Poor Law Amendment Act of 1834. The Act stated that anyone requiring public assistance could only receive it in a workhouse, not in their own home. Workhouses were to be made as unpleasant as possible, to discourage anyone from entering, and each parish, or group of parishes, was to have its own workhouse, run by an elected board of guardians. As we will see, the records of these boards of guardians provide plenty of material for the family history researcher.

The administrative structure of the poor law was dismantled by the Local Government Act of 1929. This dissolved the boards of guardians and handed responsibility for caring for the poor to councils instead of workhouses. The final Poor Law Act was in 1938 and the whole poor law system was replaced by the National Assistance Act of 1948, which brought through the welfare state.

The survival of poor law records varies from town to town and, even where they do survive, the chances of finding a relative mentioned can be slim. Most of the records relate to the regular meetings of poor law guardians. These are very interesting for background research, as they usually covered workhouse business such as food and clothing, but do not often mention individual residents. However, if your ancestor was unfortunate enough to have fallen foul of the system and been punished, they may be mentioned in the records.

If you are unsure which workhouse your ancestor stayed in, or which workhouses existed in that person's area, trade directories for a town list all poor law unions and workhouses, giving you a starting point for your research. Local record offices often have minute books which relate to the weekly or fortnightly meetings the guardians held. Many newspapers carried reports on the meetings held by the board of guardians, to which members of the press were sometimes invited.

The meetings discussed matters such as when the workhouse building was being altered, and gave details of costs and the structure of the alterations. There can also be information about members of staff who had been taken on or who were leaving and information about how much they were paid.

Census returns covered workhouses and it was usually the head of the workhouse who provided the information about the inmates. Sometimes, just initials were given for the inmates, at other times full names, and even occupations, if they were undertaking named work in the institution.

Local newspapers often carried advertisements for workhouse officers, which listed the duties and sometimes the pay scale. Another useful source in a local newspaper can be the letters page. The administration of a local workhouse was often an issue of heated debate. The workhouse may have reached the news pages if there was a fire, an accident, or scandal.

The website www.workhouses.org.uk is an excellent source of information about all aspects of life in the workhouse and also provides a comprehensive introduction to the history of workhouses and poor laws. The site features a section devoted to the location of workhouses throughout the UK. There are dozens of listings for Yorkshire. Selecting the East Riding brings up ten locations, one of which is Driffield. The Driffield page includes photographs of the town's workhouse and how the site now looks, a listing of the staff and inmates of the workhouse from the 1881 census and a history of how the workhouse came to be built.

Chapter 10

DIRECTORY OF ARCHIVE REPOSITORIES AND FAMILY HISTORY SOCIETIES

This chapter provides contact details for all of the archive repositories that have been mentioned in this book. In most cases, archives, museums and sometimes libraries require you to make an appointment before visiting. You may also be required to bring along forms of identification, for security purposes, before being allowed to view material. Making an appointment works to your benefit, as it ensures someone is on hand to help with your enquiries and it is often possible to arrange for specific material to be waiting for you. All contact details are correct at the time of going to press. You are advised to check these with the organization before visiting.

ARCHIVES
North Yorkshire

Borthwick Institute of Historical Research
St Anthony's Hall, Peasholme Green, York, YO1 7PW; tel. 01904 642315;
www.york.ac.uk/inst/bihr
One of the UK's most important archives, now housed in purpose-built premises at the University of York. The institute specializes in ecclesiastical archives, but has thousands of other records relating to the city of York and the wider county. Most of the wills proven in Yorkshire can be found here, alongside the records of many important York-based businesses, including Rowntrees of York.

North Yorkshire County Record Office
County Hall, Northallerton, DL9 3EL; tel. 01609 777585;
www.northyorks.gov.uk
The North Yorkshire County Record Office holds many of the records relating to the historic North Riding of the county. Millions of documents are held and the office also offers conservation and reprographic services.

South Yorkshire

Barnsley Archives
Barnsley Archives and Local Studies Department, Barnsley Metropolitan Borough Council, Barnsley Central Library, Shambles St, Barnsley, S70 2JF; tel. 01226 773950; www.barnsley.gov.uk
Barnsley Archives is based at the Barnsley Central library and holds thousands of items relating to the history of the area, including title deeds, photographs of the local area, wills, maps and newspapers.

A useful collection is the Burlands Annals, a chronology of events in Barnsley and the surrounding area for 1744–1864, compiled by John Hugh Burland. There is also a collection of Yorkshire-interest books and pamphlets, and a collection of books by local authors.

Doncaster Archives
King Edward Road, Balby, Doncaster, DN4 0NA; tel 01302 859811;
www.doncaster.gov.uk
The archives hold over 800 years worth of records and among the most important sets of documents are the Doncaster Borough Charters, dating between 1194 and 1836. These record rights granted to the borough by monarchs throughout this period, rights which often had a big impact on the people of the area. The final charter in the collection for 1836, for example, deals with King William IV restoring the right of Doncaster to holds its own quarter sessions in the town.

Sheffield Archives
52 Shoreham St, Sheffield, S1 4SP; tel. 0114 2039395; www.sheffield.gov.uk
The records of Sheffield archives date from the twelfth century and include material relating to the city itself and parts of South Yorkshire and North Derbyshire. There is information about landed estates in the area, the city's parks and rural areas, as well as archives on religion, charities and voluntary organizations, hospitals and schools.

East Yorkshire

East Riding of Yorkshire Archives Service
Treasure House, Champney Road, Beverley, HU17 9BA; tel. 01482 392790; www.eastriding.gov.uk
The service holds archives from the twelfth century to the present day, relating to all East Riding communities. The material ranges from parchment rolls to electronic records. The service has recently launched an online catalogue which features all records held by the archives and which summarizes all its collections, giving descriptions of individual documents.

The archives are closed until early 2007. Check the website for details of reopening.

Hull City Archives
79 Lowgate, Hull, HU1 1HN; tel. 01482 615102; www.hullcc.gov.uk
Particularly strong on local industries including trawling and shipbuilding. The archives are due to combine with Hull Local Studies Library and Hull University Library in 2009. Details will be released on the website once they have been confirmed.

Hull University Archives
University of Hull, Hull, HU6 7RX; tel. 01482 465265; www.hull.ac.uk
A collection of over 750,000 documents dating from the eleventh century onwards. The collections are particularly strong on landed family and estate records. These include estate correspondence, wills and marriage settlements, manorial records from the fourteenth century onwards and several complete runs of court rolls for the area.

The university also holds archives for dozens of pressure groups who campaigned about various causes, including the Beverley Minster Open Spaces Campaign and the Housewives' League.

West Yorkshire

West Yorkshire Archive Service, Bradford
Bradford Central Library, Princes Way, Bradford BD1 1NN; tel. 01274 731931; www.wyjs.org.uk
The Bradford office contains records for estates including the Busfield Ferrands of St Ives, Bingley and the Tempests of Tong Hall. These estate records include manorial court rolls, title deeds, estate surveys and household accounts. The Bradford archives are registered by the diocese of Bradford as a place for records to be deposited. Nonconformity was also strong in this area and the holdings of the Bradford office reflect this.

Also available to researchers are the Bradford Council records, and those of

The Wakefield headquarters of the West Yorkshire Archive Service.

its predecessor bodies, including the Bradford Borough Council. These types of records include minute books and reports, rate books, building plants, registers of teachers and inmates of welfare institutions.

West Yorkshire Archive Service, Calderdale
Central Library, Northgate House, Northgate, Halifax, HX1 1UN; tel. 01422 392636; www.archives.wyjs.org.uk
Some of the most important estate records held include those of the Listers of Shibden Hall, Stansfelds of Field House and Sunderlands of Coley Hall. Many of these documents relate to medieval times and the Shibden Hall documents include eye-witness accounts of battles during the American War of Independence. The office holds parish records of Shelf, as well as archives for over 200 Nonconformist churches, including Baptists, Congregational and Methodist.

The Halifax area is famous for its textile production and this is reflected in the collections held by the archives. These include records of John Crossley & Sons, carpet manufacturers, and Fielden Brothers of Todmorden, cotton manufacturers.

West Yorkshire Archive Service, Kirklees
Central Library, Princess Alexandra Walk, Huddersfield, HD1 2SU; tel. 01484 221966; www.wyjs.org.uk

The Kirklees branch of the West Yorkshire Archives Service is housed in Huddersfield Central Library. The office holds family and estate records for dozens of local families, including over eight hundred years of records for the Beaumont family. Also available are business records for many Kirklees firms, with a particular emphasis on textile holdings, reflecting the predominance of the textile trade in the area. The office holds the records of the National Union of Dyers, Bleachers and Textile Workers as well as the minutes of over thirty branches of the National Co-operative Society.

West Yorkshire Archive Service, Leeds
Chapeltown Road, Sheepscar, Leeds, LS7 3AP; tel. 0113 2145814; www.archives.wyjs.org.uk

The Leeds office has wills and indexes for the eastern deaneries of the archdeaconry of Richmond and the peculiars of Knaresborough and Masham. There are records for the Leeds workhouse, but these can be patchy in their survival. They include birth, death and illegitimacy registers and emigration registers and adoption and fostering. There is a collection about the emigration of orphaned children by various social groups, also reports by the medical officers who visited children who had been placed in new homes, to see if they were being well treated. There are records for Headingley Children's Home for 1860–1983.

Tithe maps and enclosure awards give information on renting or ownership of land, including farms. There are records of labourers and service people, including wage books for servants. Among the estate archives held are those of Nostell Priory and Harewood House.

West Yorkshire Archive Service, Wakefield (Headquarters)
Registry of Deeds, Newstead Road, Wakefield, WF1 2DE; tel. 01924 305980; www.wyjs.org.uk

The Wakefield headquarters of the West Archive Service is based in the same building as the Registry of Deeds. Like the other regional record offices, it is strong on material about local businesses, institutions and places of worship.

Among records held are vehicle registration documents, which can be used to view the original papers of a vehicle, West Riding quarter sessions material and records relating to the West Riding House of Correction. There are also records for the West Yorkshire police force. Another resource are coroners' records, although these can be patchy, both in the number that have survived and in their usefulness, due to the amount of detail they may contain.

Yorkshire Archaeological Society
23 Clarendon Road, Leeds, LS2 9NZ; tel. 0113 2456362;
www.laplata.co.uk/yas/
The Yorkshire Archaeological Society, founded in 1863, exists to promote the study of Yorkshire's historical past – including the agriculture, archaeology, architecture, industry, religion and history of the people who have lived and worked in the county. The society headquarters are situated in an eighteenth-century merchant's house which has been enlarged over the years and includes an extensive library, archive and lecture room.

The society is made up of a number of special interest groups which include aerial photography, family history, industrial history, local history, medieval, prehistory, Roman antiquities. Each section has its own lecture programme, excursions and fieldwork and occasionally joins with the parent society or other societies in the area for larger meetings.

MUSEUM ARCHIVES

North Yorkshire

National Railway Museum
Leeman Road, York, YO26 4XJ; tel. 01904 686 235; www.nrm.org.uk
One of the largest collections of railways books and memorabilia in the country. Items of particular interest include details of railway accidents and information about railway construction in Yorkshire.

Yorkshire Air Museum
Halifax Way, Elvington, York, YO41 4AU; tel. 01904 608595;
www.yorkshireairmuseumco.uk
Based at a former airfield, the museum holds what is believed to be the only air gunners' collection in the UK. There is also a library of books relating to air industry.

Yorkshire Film Archive
York St John College, Lord Mayors Walk, York, YO31 7EX; tel. 01904 716550;
www.yorkshirefilmarchive.com
Over 100 years of film archive relating to life, work and religion in the county. Particularly strong on farming and industry, the film collections continue to grow and develop.

South Yorkshire

Kelham Island Museum
Alma St (off Corporation St), Sheffield, S3 8RY; tel. 0114 2722106;
www.simt.co.uk
Kelham Island Museum has been displaying and conserving items relating to the city's industrial history for over 100 years. Collections include items relating to the metallurgical, iron, steel, tool and cutlery trades which have dominated the area for centuries.

The National Fairground Archive
Main Library, University of Sheffield, Western Bank, Sheffield, S10 2TN; tel. 0114 2227231; www.shef.ac.uk/nfa
A collection of photographic, printed and manuscript material about show people and travelling fairs

East Yorkshire

Hull Maritime Museum
Queen Victoria Square, Hull, HU1 3DX; tel. 01482 613902;
www.hullcc.gov.uk
The museum's archives, based at one of Britain's foremost fishing ports, have plenty of information about Hull's development from a medieval fishing village to one of the world's leading ports and also hold rare material on the whaling industry.

West Yorkshire

Colour Museum
Perkin House, 82 Grattan Road, Bradford, BD1 2JB; tel. 01274 725138;
www.sdc.org.uk
The Colour Museum houses the archives of the Society of Dyers and Colourists. Researchers are able to view the society's archives by appointment, including photographs, artefacts and publications relating to the society's activities from 1884 onwards.

The Second World War Experience Centre
5 Feast Field (off Town St), Horsforth, Leeds, LS18 4TJ; tel. 0113 2584993;
www.war-experience.org
A collection of books, letters and memorabilia relating to the Second World War, covering both the military and civilians.

LIBRARIES

North Yorkshire

Scarborough Library
Vernon Rd, Scarborough, YO11 2NN; tel. 01723 500802;
www.northyorks.gov.uk
The library holds records dating from the twelfth century to the present day, including business, charity and hospital archives. Many of the holdings relate to the town's importance as a seaside and fishing resort. Collections include the records of the Scarborough Cliff Bridge Co. and the Promenade Pier Co., as well as Scarborough School records from 1870 to 1960.

York Library Local History and Reference Collection
York Central Library Square, Museum St, York, YO1 7DS; tel. 01904 655631; www.york.gov.uk
The library is home to the York history room which contains over 13,000 books, pamphlets and microfilm records relating to the history of York and the surrounding area. There are census returns from 1851 onwards and a parish index showing which returns are held. York parish registers are held, some transcribed, from the sixteenth to nineteenth century, and also some Roman Catholic registers. There is a York marriage index for 1701–1837. The earliest available directory for the city dates back to 1781.

York Minster is home to one of the country's oldest libraries.

York Minster Library
York Minster Library and Archives, Dean's Park, York, YO1 2JQ; tel. 01904 611118; www.yorkminster.org

The York Minster Library is the largest cathedral library in England, with over 120,000 volumes in its collections. The library's collections are particularly strong on medieval and ecclesiastical history. Among the most useful collections to family history researchers are the 'Yorkshire Collections', which comprise 20,000 books and pamphlets relating to the county, including publications on local history, playbills and Yorkshire newspapers.

The library holds a bibliographical database of the names of over half a million Yorkshire people pre-1500. A search service is available on request for a fee, with no charges made for an unsuccessful search. More details can be obtained from the above address.

South Yorkshire

Sheffield Local Studies Library
Central Library, Surrey St, Sheffield, S1 1XZ; tel. 0114 2734711; www.sheffield.gov.uk

Sheffield Local Studies Library exists to preserve and collect written, filmed and oral material about the city and surrounding areas. Visitors are able to consult over 30,000 volumes about the history of Sheffield and its people.

There is a collection of films about life in the city, and oral history recordings which feature local people talking about life in Sheffield. The library also holds over 60,000 photographs about people and places of Sheffield, which can be searched via a card index.

East Yorkshire

Beverley Local Studies Library
Treasure House, Champney Rd, Beverley, HU17 9BG; tel. 01482 881861; www.eastriding.gov.uk

Holdings include a picture playhouse collection from Beverley cinema and notebooks and diaries relating to those who emigrated from North Yorkshire to the United States. The library is closed until early 2007. Check the website for details of reopening.

Hull Central Library, Local Studies
Albion St, Hull, HU1 3TF; tel. 01482 210077; www.hullcc.gov.uk

The library holds information on whaling, once one of the city's principal industries. The whaling collection includes logbooks and journals from nineteenth-century whaling trips and statistics about the industry and its effect on the local economy.

West Yorkshire

Bradford Local Studies Reference Library
Central Library, Princes Way, Bradford, BD1 1NN; tel. 01274 433661;
www.bradford.gov.uk

The local studies library is situated on the fifth floor of Bradford Central Library and its facilities are available to all members of the public. Holdings include the 1851 census for Bradford, a card name index containing details obtained from local newspapers of those reported wounded or missing in the First World War and those service people mentioned in local newspapers during the Second World War.

The library holds local trade directories for 1792–1969 and has microfiches of Bradford Parish Church registers for 1599–1983.

Huddersfield Local Studies Library
Princess Alexandra Walk, Huddersfield, HD1 2SU; tel. 01484 221965;
www.kirklees.gov.uk

The library holds a large collection of material relating to the Kirklees area. This includes books, maps, photographs, trade directories and parish records. The Kirklees digital archive allows users to view and order over 40,000 images of the local area, from a touch screen available at the library.

J B Priestley Library
University of Bradford, Bradford, BD7 1DP; tel. 01274 235256;
www.brad.ac.uk

The J B Priestley Library is part of the University of Bradford and is particularly strong on material relating to the city's textile industry. The library also holds the archives of the Bradford Institute of Technology and the Bradford Technical College Archive.

Leeds Local Studies Library
Leeds Central Library, Calverley St, Leeds, LS1 3AB; tel. 0113 2478290;
www.leeds.gov.uk/library

The Leeds Local Studies Library is one of the largest libraries devoted to local studies in the region, with over 180,000 items available to view. The collection includes 12,000 maps, 32,000 prints (Leeds Local Studies Library section) and photographs of Leeds and surrounding areas and 6,000 playbills. Maps are available which cover all areas of Yorkshire, starting from 1500, with Ordnance Survey maps from the 1850s also at the library. The library has recently acquired microfilms of the burial registers for all Leeds municipal cemeteries, which include both burials and cremations.

Special Collections, Leeds University Library
Department of Special Collections, University of Leeds, Leeds, LS2 9JT; tel.
0113 23355188; www.leeds.ac.uk/library
The Leeds University Library Special Collections holds some of the finest and rarest books in the country. There are over 200,000 books and hundreds of thousands of manuscripts in the collections. The archives include material donated to the library over the years, including collections from Ripon Cathedral Library and the libraries of Yorkshire Quakers.

The Yorkshire Collection is of particular interest to local historians, featuring plenty of information about Yorkshire life, culture and history. Material available for consultation includes books about local and church history, guide books for the region and biographies of eminent Yorkshire people.

MISCELLANEOUS

Bradford Textile Archive

Carlton Street, Bradford, BD7 1AY; tel. 01274 753268;
www.textilearchive.bilk.ac.uk
A collection of historical textiles, patterned cards and textile journals.

North West Catholic History Society

C/o Mr J Hilton, 282 Whelley, Wigan, WN2 1DA; www.catholic-
history.org.uk/nwchs
The society promotes the study of the history of Catholicism in the north-west and produces an annual journal of research. The society has published several books aimed at historians researching Catholic history in the north of England, details of which are on the website.

Saltaire Studies Centre

2nd Floor, Exhibition Building, Exhibition Road, Saltaire, Shipley, BD18 3JW;
tel. 01274 327225; www.shipley.ac.uk
A unique collection of books, Salt family memorabilia and information on Saltaire.

Harewood House Trust

Moor House, Harewood Estate, Harewood, Leeds, LS17 9LQ; tel. 0113
2181014; www.harewood.org
Holds archives relating to the Lascelles family who occupied Harewood House from the eighteenth century onwards.

Kiplin Hall

Near Scorton, Richmond, N. Yorks, DL10 6AT; tel. 01748 818178;
www.kiplinhall.co.uk
Archives include over 20 volumes relating to the history of Kiplin Hall, its interior and the people who have lived and worked there.

Church Lads' and Church Girls' Brigade Headquarters

2 Barnsley Rd, Wath Upon Dearne, Rotherham, S63 6PY; tel. 01709 876535;
www.clcgb.org.uk
Christian organisation with over 100 years of history. The brigade's headquarters house the organization's archives, which include badges, medals and file cards relating to every brigade company throughout the world.

FAMILY HISTORY SOCIETIES IN YORKSHIRE

Joining a family history for the area or areas where your ancestors came from can be an excellent way to enrich your own research. Most societies produce a quarterly journal, usually containing articles about the history of places in your chosen area and local industries and characters.

As well as holding regular meetings with talks and lectures, many of the societies also organize special events such as induction days for beginners at local record offices, computer classes for those new to internet genealogy and walks to places of local and historic interest.

The majority of societies in this list produce a list of members' interests, where each member is able to submit a list of the surnames they are researching, together with relevant dates and geographic areas of research. This can be a way for other interested researchers to get in touch and you may even make contact with distant relatives researching the same line.

North Yorkshire

City of York and District Family History Society
140 Shipton Rd, York, YO30 5RU; tel. 01904 652363;
www.yorkfamilyhistory.org.uk
The society represents the area covered by the modern archdeaconry of York. Members meet on the first Wednesday of each month (except August) and have use of a research room twice a week. The room contains microfiche and microfilm readers and computers. A dedicated member of the society is on hand to help and advise.

The society has an active monumental inscription recording team and the society's website also has links to an e-group, where members are able to exchange news and read information from committee members. The society's publications include 1851 and 1891 census indexes and the York marriage index for 1701–1837, which covers 23 York parish churches and York Minster.

Harrogate and District Family History Society
Mrs W Symington, Chairman, 18 Aspin Drive, Knaresborough, HG5 8HH
The society was part of the Ripon Historical Society, but in 2005 members decided to form two separate societies. The society holds a monthly meeting, and members are able to use the society's library, and get advice about their family history research from members of the committee before the formal meeting. The group is in the process of compiling a database of members' interests, due for completion in 2006, and sell a range of microfiche, including local parish registers plus the 1851 and 1891 census returns for the area. Publications for sale include Yorkshire Hearth Tax lists for parts of the three Yorkshire Ridings for 1672–3.

Ripon Historical Society and Family History Group
Mrs R Norris, Membership Secretary, The Rossan, Auchencairn, Castle Douglas, Kircudbrightshire, DG7 1QR; RHSinfo@aol.com
The society was founded in 1987 and covers Ripon and the surrounding area from Masham to South Stainley and from Skelton to Nidderdale. These are roughly the areas covered by the ancient Ripon Liberty and the Peculier of Masham. Meetings are held on the second Wednesday of each month (except August) at Ripon City Library. Members hear talks on a wide range of subjects and the society also organizes joint meetings and outings with the Ripon Civic Society from time to time.

The society has a sister organization, Ripon Local Studies Research Centre, in the town centre, where members are welcome to drop in for advice or to partake in self-help groups organized by the society. The research centre holds a selection of reference books to borrow and of publications to buy.

The society has been actively involved for several years in the Ripon Records Project. This ongoing project involves transferring Ripon Records on to microfilm, which are then available to the members of the public at Ripon City Library. The society has also produced Hearth Tax lists for all of the North and East Riding and York city, as well as the wapentakes of the West Riding that are not already in print. The group is also recording monumental inscriptions in the area and has transcribed and published on microfiche the Ripon Parish Registers. They also offer an indexed Calendar of Wills and Administrations proved in the Masham Peculier area. The society produces a quarterly journal *The Ripon Historian*.

Upper Dales Family History Group
Croft House, Newbiggin in Bishopdale, nr Leyburn, DL8 3TD; tel. 01969 663738; www.bishopdale.demon.co.uk
The group is a branch of the Cleveland Family History Society and covers the following areas: Apedale, Arkengarthdale, Birkdale, Bishopdale, Coverdale, Raydale, Sleddale, Swaledale, Walden, West Stonesdale, Whitsundale, Widdale and Wensleydale. The group holds regular meetings, offers an email group for members not able to attend face-to-face meetings and hosts a genealogy computer club which caters for all abilities. The club operates twelve online computers, a scanner and makes available a range of data, including the 1881 census.

South Yorkshire

Barnsley Family History Society
58a High St, Royston, Barnsley, S71 4RN; www.barnsleyfhs.co.uk
The society covers the Barnsley region, extending from Thurnscoe and Goldthorpe in the east, to Dunford Bridge in the west, and from Darton in the north, to Wortley in the south. The society offers monthly meetings and holds separate members' nights, where microfiche readers are available. A journal is published four times a year and a regular email newsletter is also sent out. There is an online register of member's surname interests. The society is involved in an ongoing project to index the 1851 Barnsley area census.

Doncaster and District Family History Society
Marton House, 125 The Grove, Wheatley Hills, Doncaster, DN2 5SN; tel. 01302 367257; www.doncasterfhs.freeserve.co.uk
The society has been established for over 25 years and is one of the largest town family history societies, covering the whole of the archdeaconry of Doncaster. The area covered stretches from Snaith and Rawcliffe in the north to Bawtry and Tickhill in the south and from Adlingfleet in the east to Wombwell in the west.

The society holds a monthly meeting at the Doncaster School for the Deaf on the last Wednesday of the month (except December). Members also have free use of the Palgrave Research Centre (subject to an annual review). The society have produced more than 210 publications including the full 1851 census, and burial index for churches and churchyards for the whole archdeaconry. Also available are thirteen CDs including the 1871 census and 1881 census, with the 1891 census series next to be published. There is an annual family history day on the last weekend of October which offers speakers, help and advice, searches and book stalls.

Grenoside and District Local History Group
4 Stepping Lane, Grenoside, Sheffield, S35 8RA; tel. 0114 2456959;
www.grenosidelocalhistory.co.uk

The group has over seventy members and offers a varied programme including workshop mornings where the group's archive collection can be accessed by both members and non-members, and group outings to places of historical interest. The archive collection consists of photographs of the village and its people, information, books and other items of historical interest relating to the village, occupations, etc. These are continually being added to and members welcome any additional information. Any photographs people have of the area can be scanned by the group to add to their collection. The group also have a fascinating collection of cuttings from a local newspaper, the *Hoyland, Chapeltown, Penistone and Stocksbridge Express*. These were written and collected by Mr T W Fulleylove in the earlier part of the last century.

Whilst the group cannot undertake research, they do welcome enquiries and if people are unable to visit on a workshop morning to do their own research, they will endeavour to help provide photos and census data in return for a small donation to cover their costs.

Rotherham Family History Society
7 St Stephen's Rd, Rotherham, S65 1PJ; www.rotherhamfhs.f9.co.uk

The society meets monthly, and also holds separate workshops and open evenings where members can search society databases and CDs on the society's computers. Projects include recording monumental inscriptions in local cemeteries and transcribing census records. The society produces a quarterly journal *A Bridge in Time* and operates an enquiry service for members who live outside the Rotherham area. A wide range of publications is offered to members, including transcribed school registers, guides to the history of the area and CDs of the 1814 and 1871 Rotherham census.

Sheffield and District Family History Society
5 Old Houses, Piccadilly Road, Chesterfield, Derbys, S41 0EH;
www.sheffieldfhs.org.uk

The society holds monthly meetings (except August) which welcome both members and non-members. A speaker covers a topic of local interest, and then there is the opportunity to discuss family history research issues with members of the society and committee. Their journal *The Flowing Stream* is produced four times a year. The society operates an active transcriptions programme, and has recently completed the 1891 census transcription for the area. The society offers a search service of the burial indexes for around 250,000 burials in all Church of England churches in the area covered by the society, from 1813 onwards. The search service is open to anyone and details are available on the society's website.

East Yorkshire

Boothferry Family and Local History Group

17 Airmyn Avenue, Goole, DN14 6PF; email howardrj@madasafish.com

The group's main interests are Goole, Hook, Airmyn, Rawcliffe, Snaith and the Marshland villages. They meet at The Courtyard, Boothferry Road, Goole, on the second and fourth Mondays of each month (excluding Bank Holidays) and have speakers on a variety of topics connected with local history, family history and some general history. One of the summer meetings is a visit to a local village for a guided tour followed by a meal. They have a group library of books which members can borrow and hold an open day every October.

Their publications include *Goole Cemetery Monumental Inscriptions* (five volumes with a sixth in preparation) and births, marriages and deaths in Goole newspapers. Also available is the *1861 Census Index to Goole and Hook* and 1861 census indexes to surrounding villages.

East Yorkshire Family History Society

169 Beverley Rd, Hessle, HU13 9AS; tel, 01482 222262; www.eyfhs.org.uk

The society has four centres – Beverley, Bridlington, Kingston upon Hull and Scarborough – each of which hold monthly meetings (with the exception of August and December). The society's quarterly magazine *The Banyan Tree* is available to members, who also have free access to the society's research centre, adjacent to the Hull city archives. This centre offers members access to all the society's publications, use of computer terminals and fiche and microfilm readers. The society's publications include 1851 census booklets and full transcripts of parish registers.

West Yorkshire

Bradford Family History Society

2 Leaventhorpe Grove, Thornton, Bradford, BD13 3BN;
www.bradfordfhs.org.uk

The census registration district of 'Bradford, West Riding' is used as the society's geographical area of interest and covers much more than the original township of Bradford. The society produces a quarterly journal *The Bod-Kin* and holds monthly meetings and beginners evenings as well as hosting a computer group. The society operates a 'link scheme' for members who live outside the Bradford area. The scheme offers members a limited research service by a local member working on an expenses-only basis. The society has produced a full transcription of the 1851 Bradford census, which is available on CD and members are currently working on transcribing the monumental inscriptions in the city's Undercliffe cemetery.

Calderdale Family History Society incorporating Halifax and District
61 Gleanings Avenue, Norton Tower, Halifax, HX2 0NU; tel. 01422 360756;
www.users.globalnet.co.uk/~cfhs/
The society holds monthly meetings and produces a quarterly journal *The Scrivener*. The society operates a limited enquiry service for the area's parish registers and 1851 and 1881 censuses. Members are entitled to use a dedicated research room at Brighouse library, which is open twice a week and manned by trained volunteers from the society. The room offers computers and micro-fiche readers, as well as a range of library books which are available for members to borrow. The society recently published the Halifax 1851 census on CD and hopes to follow up with census returns for other towns in its catchment area.

Huddersfield and District Family History Society
15 Huddersfield Rd, Neltham, Huddersfield, HD9 4NJ; tel. 01484 852420
This caters particularly for those researching and with interests in the Metropolitan District of Kirklees. The area comprises Batley, Colne Valley, Denby Dale, Dewsbury, Huddersfield, Holme Valley, Kirkburton, Meltham, Mirfield and Spen Valley. Within its boundaries lie the eleven ancient parishes of Almondbury, Batley, Birstall, Dewsbury, Emley, Hartshead, Huddersfield, Kirkburton, Kirkheaton, Mirfield and Thornhill.

The society hosts ten meetings a year, usually on the second Tuesday of the month at Huddersfield Town Hall, as well as occasional workshop evenings and visits to places of interest. There is a quarterly journal and a library/research room for members, which is available three times a week in Meltham. The library contains hundreds of items of local and general interest including the IGI for the whole of England, Wales and Scotland on microfiche, church and place histories for the local area, exchange journals from most English family history societies, printed parish registers and how-to genealogy books.

Keighley and District Family History Society
2 The Hallows, Shann Park, Keighley, BD20 6HY; tel. 01535 672144;
www.keighleyfamilyhistory.org.uk
The society covers the town of Keighley and a wide area of West and North Yorkshire including Ingleton, Clapham, Giggleswick, Skipton, Bingley and Haworth.
Members meet monthly and also hold an annual family history fair and/or open workshop. Facilities available to members include fiches and fiche readers and a library of books and journals. Projects members have completed include monumental inscriptions and the recording of information in local censuses and parish records.

Morley and District Family History Group
19 Hawthorne Drive, Gildersome, Leeds, LS27 7YJ; www.morleyfhg.co.uk
The group meets monthly and a family history library is available to members before the meetings. Members are sent the society's journal *The Cameo* three times a year and a directory of members' interests is published annually. The group offer over eighty fiches and booklets for sale, as well as local maps and local history books. They have recently produced an index of names on war memorials in the Morley area. Also offered is a search service for burial records in the area.

Pontefract and District Family History Society
62 Wheatfield Ave, Oakes, Huddersfield, HD3 4FR; www.pontefract.fhs.co.uk
As well as Pontefract, which includes the Chapelry of Knottingley, the areas of Carleton, East Hardwick and Tanshelf, the society also covers the ancient parishes of Castleford, Ackworth, Birkin, Featherstone, Hemsworth, Kippax, Normanton, Methley, South Kirby, Ledsham, Monk Fryston, Kellington, Badsworth, Felkirk, Wragby, Darrington, Womersley, Brotherton, Ferry Fryston. Kirk Smeaton, and the towns and villages within them.

The society meets once a month and produces a quarterly journal *The Bridge*. The society lends CDs, maps and books to members and also offers a search service for members who live at a distance. The society is very active in producing research material, with over 170 booklets produced to date.

Wharfedale Family History Group
Derek Halliday, Matchless House, Draughton, Skipton, BD23 6EA; www.wfhg.org.uk
Wharfedale Family History Group hold monthly meetings at both Burley in Wharfedale and Grassington. The group's journal *The Wharfedale Newsletter* is sent to members quarterly. The group offers a library for members and also sells a wide range of family history publications, census indexes and other genealogical data. They are currently involved in a major genealogical project 'pedigrees and histories of families in the Wharfedale area', a growing database currently featuring around 70,000 names.

Wakefield and District Family History Society

32 Blenheim Rd, Wakefield, WF1 3JZ; tel. 01924 373310; www.wdfhs.co.uk

The area covered by the society is the Wakefield Metropolitan District Council: the parishes of Ackworth, Badsworth, Castleford, Crofton, Darrington, Featherstone, Felkirk, Ferry Fryston, Hemsworth, Knottingley, Normanton, Ossett, Pontefract, Sandal Magna, South Kirkby, Wakefield, Warmfield, West Bretton, Woolley, Wragby and those parts of the parishes of Thornhill and Royston which are now within the area.

The society meets once a month, and at the meetings are stalls selling the society's own publications, local books and family history guides. The society's journal *The Wakefield Kinsman* is sent to members quarterly. As well as offering various publications for sale, the society has produced a photo index of local schools, churches, chapels and pubs. There are over 500 members and the society has an active publishing programme, having published transcriptions of censuses, marriage indexes, parish registers and gravestone transcriptions.

CONCLUSION

This book has given a flavour of the many and varied records available to anyone researching their Yorkshire ancestors. There is no substitute for visiting the areas your ancestors made their home and seeing these records for yourself.

Birth, marriage and death certificates are only the bare bones of family history research. By visiting the different regions of Yorkshire and exploring the county's many archives, you can bring your ancestors closer to you than ever. So many Yorkshire people have left behind tantalizing evidence of their existence. It is all out there waiting for you to discover.

INDEX